WHAT NEXT?

By Bob Evans

All proceeds are for the
Liverpool Seafarers Centre, 20,
Crosby Road South,
Liverpool. L22 1RQ
Registered with the Charity Commission. No. 1125539

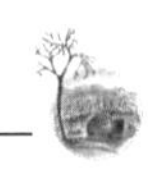

First published 2019 by LT Print Group Limited, Alfred Road, Wallasey, Wirral, CH44 7HY

British Library Cataloguing in Publication Data.
A catalogue record for this book is available from the British Library.

ISBN 978 1 9160438 1 7

Dedicated to the people who have shared their lives with me

Books by Bob Evans

A Dog Collar in the Docks

Mersey Mariners

The Way to Liverpool

The Training Ships of Liverpool

HMS EAGLET

The INDEFATIGABLE

The Mersey Mission to Seafarers

A Lantern on the Stern

Volume One The Early Years

Volume Two The Later Years

Volume Three The Story Never Ends

Volume Four Tales from the Sea

The CONWAY HEROES

Charlie the Mouse Volumes One and Two

Bobology The Real Jesus

A Welsh Boy

Reflections

Our Unseen God

Cwmtidy

Bits and Bobs

What next?

Canon Bob Evans was born in 1924 and keeps writing what he calls 'my last book. He accepts that fact that it might be just that! Bob was brought up in a small Welsh village in South Wales called Llanharan where he only spoke Welsh until he went to school where it was English only or the cane. He claims that he still learning how to manage the language. He was a fighter pilot in the Royal Air Force in wartime which was followed by five years at University. Ordained in 1950, he served in the Aberdare valley ... digging for coal, Tiger Bay in Cardiff docks ... Shirley Bassey country, Llandaff Cathedral, Cardiff ... where he learned to drink tea properly and sing Gregorian Chants, then came thirty years as Port Chaplain of Liverpool ... being taught by dockers how to communicate and a brief spell in the Parish of Rainhill ... being a proper Vicar. For sixteen years he was the RNR Chaplain in HMS EAGLET. He sort of retired in 1989 but has really never stopped. Canon Bob has been awarded an MBE for 'services to the maritime industry and Merchant Navy Medal for his contribution to maritime literature'.

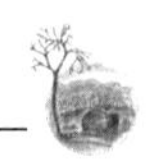

CONTENTS

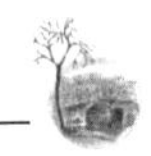

PREFACE

It must have been almost eighty years ago when, in my first term at University, I recall that with much temerity I informed the Warden of ordinands that the concept of the Resurrection made no sense to me. I expected a 'ticking off''. 'You are not alone,' he replied. 'It will all fall into place in time.' He was right and I have been given much time ... ninety-five years!

Six months back I was asked 'Can you explain to me all of this life after death nonsense?' It was a good challenge. The only material available was what I can read in scriptures with an open honest mind and a lifetime of thought. All that I ask of any reader is patience as the story unfolds and a willingness to understand with a final assurance that it all makes sense to me. It was good to write.

I have discussed the Resurrection with many friends and I thank them for their valuable contributions and often for showing little mercy with their comments. My publisher, Bob McWilliams, has above all spurred me on and without him this book would not have emerged. There are too many friends to name who have helped in the reading and corrections in this small book and all that I can do is express my thanks.

Please use patience, tolerance, love and understanding.

Bob

Thank you Joan Harley for your cover art work ... please note the crosses 'on a hill far away'.

The title 'WHAT NEXT?' seemed appropriate!

Chapter One

DID CHRIST EXIST?

In which we look at the evidence and the sources of information, non-biblical, biblical and other writings about Jesus such as the Gospel of Thomas. Jesus did exist.

My impression is that Jesus was not intent on founding a religion or that he ever hoped that someone would write down his thoughts. One of his aims was to give those about him some guidance concerning the Kingdom of Heaven. He lived in the midst of political turmoil and the people were looking for an earthly, not a heavenly kingdom. Jesus was a Jew, living with Jews, under the heel of Roman domination. His message was somewhat confused and contradictory. He did not suggest that he should be worshipped as a god … he pointed us towards a spiritual kingdom and went to some lengths to explain that we would inherit the Spirit of God.

The Jesus we think of today is barely visible in the Bible. Two thousand years of baggage has created a choice between the Christ of 'Gentle Jesus, meek and mild' and the misguided anarchist best forgotten about. Which was he? We are going to find that it is a long journey from a Galilean Jew of the first century to the concept of a risen Christ who is one with God and with us today.

There appear to be two views of Jesus. There is the Jesus of history found in the Gospels and there is the Jesus of faith, which is also in the Gospels. These views are called the 'pre-Easter Jesus' and the 'post-Easter Jesus'. The first Jesus is 'dead and gone' and hard to find; the second is alive and living in our experience. We try to separate the pre-Easter Jesus from the post-Easter Jesus … the Jesus created by faith. It is almost impossible to do this, but that is the task.

There are records apart from the New Testament. Tertullian

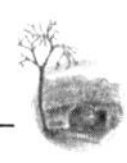

(c. AD 160–225) states in his Apologeticus … 'All these things Pilate did to Christ … he sent word of Him to the reigning Caesar, who was at that time Tiberius.'

Pliny (AD 61-114) refers to Christians in his writing and states that they 'sang hymns to Christus as if he were a god.'

Tacitus (AD 55-120) was a Roman senator and met many Christians in his courtroom. He comments on the burning of Rome during the reign of Nero. Nero fabricated scapegoats … and 'punished with every refinement the notoriously depraved Christians' (as they were popularly called). Their originator, Christ, had been executed in Tiberius's reign by the governor of Judaea, Pontius Pilate.

Suetonius (AD 75-150) and Josephus (AD 37-100) both make firm reference to the historical existence of Jesus. He is not a figment of anyone's imagination. Listen to what Josephus wrote:

'About that time lived Jesus, a wise man, if man he may be called, for he did wonderful works … a teacher of those who joyfully received the truth. He won to Himself many Jews and many Greeks. He was the Christ, and though Pilatus condemned him to death, He was our Messiah and appeared on the third day.'

There are also a large number of Christian Gospels apart from the ones that we have nominated to form the New Testament. At the end of the nineteenth century many fragments of papyrus were found in a trash heap in Egypt. The writings were more important than the scholars had first realised. They were called the Dead Sea Scrolls.

There is a remarkable interest in the modern media concerning the Dead Sea Scrolls. It makes interesting television programmes. We accept that they are possibly from the time of Jesus and as such are of value. They are manuscripts which were found in caves adjoining the Dead Sea and they reveal the religious views of the community at Qumran. The community was an exclusive and semi-monastic sect, dating from BC140 to AD 68. Since 1947 many more such scrolls have been found and they help to fill in the social and political age in which Jesus lived. The Qumran community was called the Essenes and it is probable that John the Baptist was much influenced by them and thus, in turn, they did influence Jesus. We have tended to underplay the value of John the Baptist, but I regard him as a major force in formulating the message of Jesus.

The Gospel of Thomas is of special note. It really is an early Christian document and contains one hundred and fourteen sayings of Jesus. Here is just one example.

'Jesus said, 'There was this rich person who had a great deal of money. He said 'I shall invest my money so that I may sow, reap, plant, and fill my storerooms with produce, that I may lack nothing.' These were the things he was thinking in his heart, but that night he died. Anyone here with two ears had better listen!' 63.1-3

Compare that version with Luke. 'And he told them this parable: There was a rich man whose land yielded heavy crops. He debated with himself: 'What am I to do? I have not the space to store my produce. This is what I will do,' said he. 'I will pull down my storehouses and build them bigger. I will collect in them all my corn and other goods, and then say to myself, 'Man, you have plenty of good things laid by, enough for many years: take life easy, eat, drink, and enjoy yourself.' But God said to him, 'You fool, this very night you must surrender your life; you have made your money … who will get it now?' That is how it is with the man who amasses wealth for himself and remains a pauper in the sight of God.' Luke 12.16-21

Thomas's version has simplicity with none of the moralising of Luke. His ending is abrupt and forceful; Luke makes much of the end and is almost sermonising. This clearly suggests that Thomas is a pure oral saying, but Luke has done some editing. This makes Thomas the earlier and maybe a more acceptable version. I preferred Thomas.

In fact, the Gospel of Thomas provides us with eleven parables that are also found in the first three Gospels. We cannot ignore them,

but very few Christians are aware of them.

We also have the Gospel of Peter and the Secret Gospel of Mark. There are many letters and documents. Perhaps there is no need to labour the point any longer. Accept that Jesus was a human being.

Jesus existed.

'No-one has ever seen God.' This is how St John's Gospel starts. John 1.18 Happily he continues, 'Jesus has shown us what God is like!' There are very few clues to guide us.

My quiet reflections over nine decades have convinced me that we have attributed words and deeds and expectations to Jesus that, I suspect, would surprise him. It is precisely what time does to memories … colour, expand and distort ... yet always the central core will remain. There is a punch-line to every story and that gives the story life, otherwise it would not be remembered or recorded. Jesus lived for a mere thirty years or so and we only have partial records for the few final years. And it was all rather a long time ago.

I have to find Jesus as best I can with the evidence that has remained for me to study. At least I can start somewhere. There are the Bible tales, barely remembered, often contradictory, not much more than glimpses, yet invaluable.

Probing the life of Jesus is not going to be easy. We Christians have been trained to absorb Sunday by Sunday the drama of his life and the doctrines that have evolved from them. Many Bible stories were assembled for that very purpose ... they cannot be fully trustworthy as most eyewitnesses were long dead when they were written.

Of course there are problems. I can barely remember a shopping list dictated to me half an hour before I arrive in the store, so I must take into account that the Gospel accounts were written at least thirty years after the event. It would seem that we are safer to regard them as reflections of devout minds thinking about Jesus rather than verbatim accounts. That would start to explain the inconsistencies and contradictions.

A good example of inconsistencies is found in the Resurrection story. Mark states that a young man was present when the women came to the tomb; Matthew says it was an angel; Luke says it was two men; John says two angels. It is the same in our press reports in our daily newspapers and on television. Each report is different, yet there will usually be a kernel of truth.

There are rather obvious contradictions … or are they just isolated recollections which inevitably can lead to confusion? The passage about the sheep (the good) and the goats (the bad) in Matthew states that Jesus will turn to those on his left-hand … the goats … and say, 'Depart from me ye cursed into the eternal fire which is prepared for the devil and his angels because when I was hungry, ye gave me no meat.' Matthew 25.41-43 Not much evidence of love there! But Luke says that when Jesus was not just hungry, but was being put to death, he said, 'Father, forgive them for they know not what they do'. Luke 23.34 There is an apparent contradiction between these two statements! I suspect that we might conclude that the former is just a story to illustrate a point and the latter hard and cruel fact. So both memories are to be accepted.

A brief snap-shot of how the Gospels came into being is essential to our search for the real Jesus and the resurrection story. The first three Gospels, Matthew, Mark and Luke, are interdependent … we call them the Synoptic Gospels because they reflect the same view of Jesus. The fourth, John, stands almost in isolation and is more of a meditation.

Matthew and Luke certainly use almost the whole of Mark as a prime source, almost word for word as written. Matthew had material peculiar to his Gospel as also did Luke. We are convinced that there is an unknown source (Q). This leaves us with six sources of information about Jesus … Mark, Q, Matthew, M (special Matthean

material), Luke and L (special Lucan material). Also then there is the seventh source, the Gospel of John.

It is postulated that there was a document, as yet unfound, consisting mainly of the sayings of Jesus, conventionally called Q (from the German Quelle, 'source'.) Q was probably written in AD 50 and modern scholars have 'put it together' from the material found in Matthew and Luke, but not in Mark. Mark knew nothing about the Q document. There are about two hundred verses, obviously copied from a written work and found in Matthew and Luke. They are a collection of teaching materials attributed to Jesus with hardly any narrative.

It is often forgotten that the earliest author in the New Testament was Paul. His letters were all written before the Gospels, maybe twenty years before Mark, but as Paul says very little about Jesus, he is not a major source in the search for the historical Jesus.

Did Jesus actually exist or is he a fabrication of human minds? What if the whole business about the origins of Christianity is a lie! The publication of Holy Blood, Holy Grail, the machinations of The Da Vinci Code, the postulation of a marriage between Jesus and Mary Magdelene, have all created a world-wide controversy. 'Mr. and Mrs. Jesus Christ' made rather a good sound-bite in the news. Jesus was back in the newspapers! Many people who had dismissed the Gospels as mumbo jumbo were aroused to ask questions about Jesus and Christianity and all that business recorded some two thousand years ago. Many thought that, at last, they could put these Christian myths back into the time where they come from and forget them. It had nothing to do with them today!

The quest for the historical Jesus has dominated scholars since the eighteenth century and we are still looking … it is proving to be an exciting search.

We cannot emphasise enough the fact that Jesus lived in a time of great social change and tension. The Romans had taken charge some sixty years before the birth of Jesus. There were numerous revolts against the occupying force and some forty years after his death Jerusalem and the Temple were destroyed in AD 70 This literally destroyed the world that Jesus had lived in and was a watershed in Jewish history. This surely led the early followers to grasp the message of Jesus as the way ahead ... maybe all that they had left was a kingdom in heaven! Any concept of a kingdom on earth had been removed. Our four Gospels were written against a background of failure, political turmoil and anti-Jewish backlash. The Jewish world had been shattered.

Jesus probably wrote nothing and all our evidence rests on an oral tradition. It must be said that we have no single story of Jesus that has not been processed through a believing congregation.

Probably Jesus spoke in Galilean Aramaic and the Gospels are written in Greek. Translating from one language to another is notoriously difficult. Aramaic words often have a double meaning and the Greek translation might be in error. Then add to all of this that we read an English translation of the Greek, which many people think are the actual words of God!

Whilst we really have no spoken words of Jesus, (ipsissima verba), which are not 'second hand', there may be one exception and it is very important to our understanding of Jesus. The everyday use by him of the Aramaic word 'abba' can only be pure Jesus-talk. He addressed God as 'abba'. The word 'abba is the speech of children ... Daddy! This is a Jesus word. In the time of Jesus, children would use 'abba' to address their fathers with love. Jesus felt a love-relationship with God and 'abba' expressed just that. This was the love affair of Jesus.

How do we remember? A happy event today will remind me of a happy event fifty years ago. You can even recall conversations, smells, colour, but rarely dates! However, there is always something that triggers that memory. Something happened ... what was it? That is a fair question. There must be a truth behind each memory. We

may never find the Jesus we are searching for, but that he is there is not in doubt.

If there is doubt about his existence, the Resurrection Story is of no value.

I trust that we now accept that Jesus was not a fictional character. There is so much more proof available ... over a thousand pieces are in existence. You may question the idea of God, but there is no doubt that Jesus lived.

Chapter Two

WHO WAS JESUS ?

Was his birth miraculous or was he a man like me? Is the Christmas story of any value to us? How did the thoughts of his divinity evolve? Was there an immaculate conception? Did Jesus see himself as a man or God on earth?

I wonder whether Jesus was ever told about the strange events surrounding his birth … I suspect the answer is negative. Jesus never talked about his childhood and the remarkable accounts of his birth. One person asked me a good question recently ... 'I wonder what happened to the gold and frankincense and myrrh?' Did they actually exist?

Father Christmas with all his tinsel and commercial mayhem has rather obscured the Gospel story. Some may think that the razzmatazz makes life easier for Christians. At least it is a popular happening. Everyone enjoys Christmas! I once heard someone say 'The trouble with Christmas is that they keep bringing religion into it!' But there are, without doubt, problems about Christmas for Christians.

The birth narratives in Matthew and in Luke differ from one another and are overgrown by legends and by Jewish and Christian conceptions of what they thought might have happened. The story just grew and grew and now we have fully commercialised it.

There is an enormous gap between what we proclaim in our Churches at Christmastide in the name of institutionalised Christianity and the record which we find in the two Gospels. There are no camels for the wise men, no stable or animals. The stories have grown over the centuries in the telling and, maybe as long as we accept them for what they are, there is little harm done. It is all part of building up the story to prove that Jesus was divine.

Without Matthew 1–2 and Luke 1–2 we would know nothing about the Christmas story. John has no need of it and neither does Paul nor Mark.

The statement that he was born of the 'Virgin' Mary must be questionable! Is the miraculous birth of Jesus a fact? Or is it a fable that has won acceptance and grew in volume. The early Christians began to think of him as God and 'worked' on his divinity. They searched the scriptures for signs. Was it based on scripture?

I was taught that you must believe in Christmas if you are a Christian! If you don't, you are not one. Others will insist that the divinity of Christ demands the Virgin Birth and that it is essential to the understanding of Christ. Others will suggest that the Virgin Birth denies the humanity of Christ … he is not like us and, therefore, we cannot walk in his footsteps.

Perhaps, we should just suspend our judgement because the birth stories have little, if any, bearing upon the teaching of Jesus or upon his death. In other words, if Mark, John and Paul show no interest in the Christmas story, why should we? Does the Christmas story add anything to our faith? Is it essential?

We can accept that Jesus' father was a carpenter and that probably Jesus followed the same trade. Incidentally, the Aramaic word for carpenter can also mean a wise man or a scholar or a stone-mason, but let us stay with carpenter. His parents were called Joseph and Mary. We have the names of his brothers … James, Joses, Judas and Simon. Mark 6.3 It is also stated that Jesus had sisters. Jesus spoke Galilean Aramaic. Hebrew was also understood and must have been used when discussing the scriptures with the Rabbis. He also probably managed some Greek as it was the language used in administration and commerce.

Yet he was different

'Therefore the Lord himself will give you a sign. Look, the

young woman (in Greek, a virgin) is with child and shall bear a son, and shall name him Immanuel'. Isaiah 7 14

One way to attack Jesus was to insult him. He was called a bastard. The people of Nazareth had tolerated the young man, but in their eyes he was making blasphemous claims. They had to drive this apostate from his native town. What better way than to insult him with the name Jeshua ben Miriam? ... Jesus born of Mary.

Traditionally Christian dogma tells us to accept that Jesus is the son of Mary, not of Joseph. Christians are expected to go further and believe that he was begotten by an act of the Divine Creator. However, the Jews of his day saw Mary as adulterous. Out of this came a struggle in the lifetime of Jesus. 'Is not this the carpenter, the son of Mary?' Mark 6.3 Again, one cannot ignore the fact that neither Mark nor John mentioned the Virgin Birth and that there is no reference to it by Paul. We must remember that the story did not really emerge until the end of the first century by which time Mary was dead.

If there was a miraculous birth, Jesus had a head start on me and on the rest of us. How can I be like him when he is not born like me? In fact, the idea that there was a divine act involved in the incarnation was late.

There were no text books, no body of pre-conceived doctrines and no creeds in the early church. Thoughts about Jesus were not fixed and were ever changing. There was no 'faith which was once for all delivered to the saints'. Therefore we should not feel guilty about our pursuit of the 'truth'. We are allowed to question and ponder.

Paul is our first source of information about Jesus and was probably writing some twenty years after the death of Jesus. He was obviously deeply moved by his Christ-experience on the road to Damascus.

'We preach Christ crucified … Christ the power of God and the wisdom of God.' 1 Corinthians 1.23-24

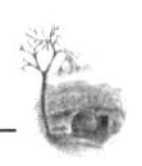

Paul sees God in Christ, not divinity or incarnation. Paul homes in on the Easter experience and apparently knows nothing of the stories surrounding the Virgin Birth. He totally accepted the resurrection story and takes it as his basis for finding God in Christ. Even if he was aware of the Christmas saga, he does not refer to it.

Thirty years or so after the death of Christ, we have the Gospel of Mark. This was the first time that we have available to us a life of Jesus in chronicle form. He opens with the words ... 'The beginning of the gospel (good news) of Jesus Christ ... the Son of God.' He explains how these words were first heard at the baptism of Jesus by John the Baptist. The voice of God spoke from heaven ... 'This is my beloved son in whom I am well pleased'. This was the start of what has become the traditional story of Jesus.

Some ten or twenty years later after Mark, the thoughts about the divine origins of Jesus have moved on. Matthew now produces birth stories. He quotes five passages from the Old Testament which he correlates with the events in his story to be 'according to the scriptures'. A study of those passages shows that they were not predictions of the future, but Matthew wanted them to portray just that.

An example is that the pronouncement of the divinity is now placed in the mouth of an angel who appeared to Joseph in a dream. The divine nature was thus pre-ordained and fulfils the words of Isaiah.

'The spirit of the Lord God is upon me because the Lord has anointed me.'....Isaiah 61.1

Matthew traces the genealogy from David to Joseph ... so how can he write that Joseph was not the father? He provides us with a table of the birth line of Jesus Christ ... son of David, son of Abraham, to Joseph, the husband of Mary, who gave birth to Jesus called Messiah.

Joseph was apparently descended from a good family and his birth was traced back to David, a founder of the royal Jewish house

and very much a pillar of Judaism. Paul agrees with this.

'On the human level he was born of David's stock, but on the level of the spirit he was declared Son of God with full powers from the time when he rose from the dead.'....Romans 1.33

Further, the statement of Paul who spoke about a 'spirit of holiness' is now changed by Matthew. 'Spirit of Holiness' now becomes the 'Holy Spirit'. This is hinting at the emerging doctrine of the Holy Trinity. At this point there is no mention of the Holy Spirit as a separate power. But Matthew has moved to the idea of the Virgin Birth induced by the 'Holy Spirit'.

Next Luke tightens up the images. He includes hymn language which reflect the Jewish Bible. The annunciating angel is given a name and appears in person and not in a dream. The annunciation was to Mary and not to Joseph and the baby was designated as both the 'Son of God' and the 'Son of the Highest'. By the year AD 100 or so, Jesus' identity with God was complete and that identification is finally placed before the conception and the birth. We have moved to the pre-existence of Christ as God and into the obscure realms of Christian theology such as we have today.

When John came to his Gospel, he omitted all birth stories even though by this time they were legion. Twice he calls Jesus the 'son of Joseph' as though he had no time for Virgin Birth stories. In fact, John goes further and talks of two births as necessary ... one was the natural birth and the other was the spiritual birth.

'In truth, in very truth I tell you, unless a man has been born over again he cannot see the Kingdom of God. 'But how is it possible', said Nicodemus, 'for a man to be born when he is old? Can he enter his mother's womb a second time and be born?' Jesus answered, 'In truth I tell you, no one can enter the Kingdom of God without being born from water and spirit. Flesh can give birth only to flesh; it is spirit that gives birth to spirit'. John .3.4-6

John sees Jesus as the light coming into this world. Mark places the coming of the 'light' at the baptism of Jesus. Matthew traces the 'light' coming down through the ages from Abraham to Jesus … chosen by God. Luke goes further back than Matthew to Adam … back to the creation of man. John goes back to God in the sense that everything goes back to God. God is in Jesus and God is in mankind. This is the light that can never be extinguished. Jesus is the Word of God … Jesus is the mind of God. Another way to understand the purpose of John is to state that the mind of God became man. God is in us.

From that point in time, the doctrines began to pile up until creeds were produced and reproduced and revised. This enabled the 'divinely appointed church' to declare the ultimate faith … accept it or be damned.

What was the point of all this? Was it to prove the divinity of Jesus?

Look again at the evidence. Matthew and Luke start their stories with the suggestion that He was conceived by the Holy Spirit, which could be another way of saying that Jesus was a spirit person. Paul never mentions the family except to say that He was 'born of woman', Galatians 4.4 ... and that according to the flesh he was descended 'from the house of David'. Romans 1.3

Mark, the earliest Gospel, has no mention of a supernatural birth, but mentions Mary twice and not in over-flattering tones. 'Is not this the carpenter, the son of Mary, the brother of James and Joseph and Judas and Simon? Are not his sisters here with us?' Mark 6.3 That was an insult from someone in the crowd. When He started his ministry, the family was not pleased. 'They set out to take charge of him, for the people were saying 'He is out of his mind.' ' Mark 3.21 There is no great maternal love in the Gospel. Mark apparently had no knowledge of the stories of the birth of Jesus and of the sanctity of Mary. The theory is that Peter in Rome dictated his memoirs to Mark, which suggests that Peter had no time for the Christmas story

Matthew built the virgin concept out of a mistranslation of Isaiah 7.14 ... the young woman (in Greek, a virgin) ... and Luke built on it. They did their research well. The wise men came from Isaiah 60 and accounted for the camels and the gold and incense. Numbers gave us the star episode. Numbers 24.17 The angel of the Lord showed the way. The shepherds came from David's association with Bethlehem … the shepherd boy who became a king. Luke actually uses a Greek word that means a 'room' rather than an inn and there is no mention of a stable. The Song of Mary … the Magnificat … is an adaptation of the song of Hannah in 1 Samuel 2.1-10. We could go on and on.

This is all understandable. In Jesus, mankind felt the presence of God. In some way this had to be accounted for. For them God lived above the bright blue sky! Therefore there had to be a 'happening'. And they found ample sacred traditions in the scriptures to back their thoughts. We all seek an explanation for what we cannot understand.

In reality, the story brings unbelievers into our church at least once a year and we all rather enjoy the tableau that bears little reference to what is written in the Gospels. In spite of all of that, I thoroughly enjoy Christmas. After all, all little boys are the same!

Whilst the birth stories seem almost absurd, it is understandable how they emerged in time and became our commercial Christmas story. Many do not believe them. However, nothing can remove the fact that Jesus had a remarkable closeness to God.

Jesus was a man,

inspired by God

Chapter Three

GOLGOTHA

In which we look at the death of Jesus. Why did they crucify him? The game of politics and the hostility of the Jewish leaders. Was Judas a traitor? Did Peter betray Jesus by denying all knowledge of his master? The death on the cross and why he died.

The certainty had gone. He took Peter, James and John … the inner circle … with him and could not conceal his distress at what lay ahead. He needed to pray.

As a child I was taught in Sunday School a little jingle about prayer, which has never failed me.

'When I pray, I speak to God,

When I listen, God speaks to me.'

I wonder whether Jesus was taught much the same in his childhood synagogue in Nazareth. That is where he was taught and studied the Scriptures.

Jesus needed to pray. When he addressed God, he called him 'Abba'. That could be translated as 'Daddy'. And remember that Peter was there and he heard the word used. When the chips were down, it was a cry from the heart. 'Daddy, Father, take this cup away from me! You can do that! But … not what I want, but what you want!'

However, Jesus knew what he had to do. 'You can carry on sleeping now, it no longer matters … get up, let's go!' There were to be darker moments ahead for Jesus, far darker than we can begin to understand. Jesus was going to feel 'God-forsaken'. He was to feel deserted by his father. He had already told his disciples that they would abandon him and he now was to face the ultimate dereliction ... it was his battle, totally abandoned by all.

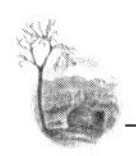

Every ounce of my being asks 'Why? How can anyone ask this of anyone? Where is love? How can a God of Love allow this betrayal?' I am struggling to find the answer.

Gethsemane was the final throw of the dice. I believe that Jesus could have walked away from it all. He had to make a decision. The agony was evident. It led to the resurrection.

'After singing the Passover Hymn, they went out to the Mount of Olives. And Jesus said, 'You will all fall from your faith; for it stands written: 'I will strike the shepherd down and the sheep will be scattered.' Nevertheless, after I am raised again I will go on before you into Galilee.' Peter answered, 'Everyone else may fall away, but I will not.' Jesus said, 'I tell you this: today, this very night, before the cock crows twice, you yourself will disown me three times.' But Peter insisted and repeated: 'Even if I must die with you, I will never disown you. And they all said the same.'

'When they reached a place called Gethsemane, he said to his disciples, 'Sit here while I pray.' And he took Peter and James and John with him. Horror and dismay came over him, and he said to them, 'My heart is ready to break with grief; stop here, and stay awake.' Then he went forward a little, threw himself on the ground, and prayed that, if it were possible, this hour might pass him by. 'Abba, Father', he said, 'all things are possible to thee; take this cup away from me. Yet not what I will, but what thou wilt.'

'He came back and found them asleep; and he said to Peter, 'Asleep, Simon? Were you not able to keep awake for one hour? Stay awake, all of you; and pray that you may be spared the test: the spirit is willing, but the flesh is weak.' Once more he went away and prayed. On his return he found them asleep again, for their eyes were heavy; and they did not know how to answer him. The third time he came and said to them, 'Still sleeping? Still taking your ease? Enough! The hour has come. The Son of Man is betrayed to sinful men. Up, let us go forward! My betrayer is upon us.' Suddenly, while he was still

speaking, Judas, one of the Twelve, appeared, and with him was a crowd armed with swords and cudgels, sent by the chief priests, lawyers, and elders. Now the traitor had agreed with them on a signal.'

'The one I kiss is your man; seize him and get him safely away.' When he reached the spot, he stepped forward at once and said to Jesus, 'Rabbi', and kissed him. Then they seized him and held him fast. One of the party drew his sword, and struck at the High Priest's servant, cutting off his ear. Then Jesus spoke: 'Do you take me for a bandit, that you have come out with swords and cudgels to arrest me? Day after day I was within your reach as I taught in the temple, and you did not lay hands on me. But let the scriptures be fulfilled.' Then the disciples all deserted him and ran away. Among those following was a young man with nothing on but a linen cloth. They tried to seize him; but he slipped out of the linen cloth and ran away naked.' Mark 14.26-52

That is a graphic account and smacks of reality. I believe that it was almost an eye witness account ... Peter talking to Mark. It is probable that the young man who escaped naked leaving his cloak behind was Mark himself. The other Gospels do not mention the incident, which surely adds nothing to the story except a personal touch. 'I was there! I saw it all.' It cannot be proved. It has been suggested that this Gospel was dictated to Mark by Peter and you can almost sense the tension as the tale was told yet again. Peter also makes it a personal testimony. All of this writing has the ring of truth. Peter is recalling what actually happened and Mark adds his personal touch. 'Among those following was a young man with nothing on but a linen cloth. They tried to seize him; but he slipped out of the linen cloth and ran away naked.' We can assume that that was Mark's addition, because it adds nothing to the story.

Why did Judas betray Jesus? Judas had lived with the disciples for three years and was certainly trusted because he was the appointed treasurer of the group. Why betray for thirty pieces of silver! He knew

Jesus and never put a foot wrong with him. There is an explanation. Judas was from the northern side of Israel and all the rest were from the south and this might have made him feel not quite part of the team. This happens with folk from Yorkshire and Lancashire and North and South Welshmen. But that is not enough. Judas, like all the disciples, had never quite grasped the purpose of Jesus. As we have seen, they all thought that Jesus was talking about the Kingdom on earth and the status of their occupied country. Judas recognised the power of Jesus and was frustrated by the events about him. If he could put pressure on Jesus surely he would act and see off the Romans and free Israel. Therefore Judas thought that he could force Jesus to take action. The betrayal would do just that. He certainly could not discuss his plan with the other disciples and never dreamt that Jesus would allow the arrest to be implemented. Judas got it wrong and he was distraught at what he had done.

'When Judas, who had betrayed him, saw that Jesus was condemned, he was seized with remorse and returned the thirty pieces of silver to the chief priests and the elders. 'I have sinned', he said, 'for I have betrayed innocent blood'.

'What is that to us?' they replied. 'That's your responsibility.'

So Judas threw the money into the temple and left. Then he went away and hanged himself.

Matthew 27ff

The story now moved on to the high priest, the elders and the scribes and Peter followed them at a distance ... listening. The inevitable question was asked by the Jewish hierarchy.

'Are you the Messiah, the Son of the Blessed One? Why do we need more witnesses? But he kept silence; he made no reply. Again the High Priest questioned him: 'Are you the Messiah, the Son of the Blessed One?' Jesus said, 'I am and you will see the Son of Man seated on the right hand of God and coming with the clouds of heaven.' Then

the High Priest tore his robes and said, 'Need we call further witnesses? You have heard the blasphemy. What is your opinion?' Their judgement was unanimous: that he was guilty and should be put to death.' Mark 14.63-65

Actually, Jesus had not committed a capital offence. The real offence in the eyes of the accusers was his attack on the Temple and all that it stood for. Even the claim that he was the Messiah was in their terms all part of his delusions. As far as they were concerned there was no way in which he was the Messiah. It was laughable. The Messiah would come in glory and wonder and triumph. This man was different. Yet he talked about a Kingdom .... and that would lead to his downfall. If the Roman governor was informed that here was a rebel who was trying to set himself up as a king, there was only one outcome ... crucifixion. The political game could be played and get Rome to sort him out.

But what about Peter? I believe that he was a brave man. The rest of the disciples had gone into hiding. They must have begun to wonder what it had all been about. The betrayal by Judas, the soldiers, the arrest, the accusations, it was all going to end in one way. The streets were now dangerous. The disciples were afraid for their lives.

Peter had other thoughts. Someone had to find out what was afoot. Of course it would be dangerous. I suspect that he pulled his cloak about him and ventured into the courtyard of the high priest's house. He actually heard the exchanges between the high priest and Jesus and remembered them well. He moved as close as possible and in the light of a brazier he was recognised by a servant girl.

'Meanwhile Peter was still in the courtyard downstairs. One of the High Priest's serving-maids came by and saw him there warming himself. She looked into his face and said, 'You were there too, with this man from Nazareth, this Jesus.' But he denied it: 'I know nothing', he said; 'I do not understand what you mean.' Then he went outside into the porch; and the maid saw him there again and began to say to the bystanders, 'He is one of them'; and again he denied it. Again, a little later, the bystanders said to Peter, 'Surely you are one of them. You must be; you are a Galilean.' At this he broke out into curses, and with an oath he said, 'I do not know this man you speak of.' Then the cock crew a second time; and Peter remembered how Jesus had said to him, 'Before the cock crows twice you will disown me three times.' And he burst into tears.' Mark 14.67-71

The game was up. He remembered the words of Jesus and it broke his heart. Of course he had denied all knowledge of Jesus and hated saying it. What else could he have done? He had hung around for as long as possible. It was time to leave.

So he went back to the other disciples to tell his story. It had been a fearful experience to see his master mocked and belittled and it was true, he had denied all knowledge of his Lord. Yet Jesus had prepared him for it and Peter was man enough to accept his failure, even though his intentions had been correct. Peter never forgot what he had seen and heard.

'When morning came the chief priests, having made their plan with the elders and lawyers and all the Council, put Jesus in chains; then they led him away and handed him over to Pilate. Pilate asked him, 'Are you the King of the Jews?' He replied, 'The words are yours.' And the chief priests brought many charges against him. Pilate questioned him again: 'Have you nothing to say in your defence? You see how many charges they are bringing against you.' But, to Pilate's astonishment, Jesus made no further reply.'

'At the festival season the Governor used to release one prisoner at the people's request. As it happened, the man known as Barabbas was then in custody with the rebels who had committed crimes. 'Do you wish me to release for you the king of the Jews?' For he knew it was out of spite that they had brought Jesus before him. But the chief priests incited the crowd to ask him to release Barabbas rather than Jesus. Pilate spoke to them again: 'Then what shall I do with the man

you call king of the Jews?' They shouted back, 'Crucify him!' 'Why, what harm has he done?' Pilate asked. They shouted all the louder, 'Crucify him!' So Pilate, in his desire to satisfy the mob, released Barabbas to them; and he had Jesus flogged and handed him over to be crucified.' Mark 15

There were thousands of crosses in the Roman world and there were thousands more after the death of Jesus. You did not have to commit much of a crime to win a cross. There was no need for much of a trial. It was more a sport than a legal transaction. One more crucifixion would not matter. The aim was to get the season of Passover done and dusted so that life could carry on. This crucifixion was not in the least important. Who cared!

The charge? Six times Mark spells it out … 'The King of the Jews'. This was pure politics, but not terribly important and of no danger to Rome. Pilate did not even attempt to arrest any of the so-called followers of this criminal. They were not dangerous enough. He thought it was just Jewish political nonsense and really nothing to do with him. Pilate knew it was a futile accusation … there was no revolt. This man was not dangerous. It was all words. This man was innocent. There was a way to avoid the problem. Barabbas got Pilate off the hook. The crowd fell for it and Pilate could wash his hands of the whole affair. It was not very important anyway.

Incidentally, there is a fable that Barabbas turned up at the crucifixion and said 'He dies for me ... I will live for him.' That's good pulpit material, but in reality I suspect that he was sitting in a tavern in his cups celebrating with his mates. He had got away with it.

'Then the soldiers took him inside the courtyard (the Governor's headquarters) and called together the whole company. They dressed him in purple, and having plaited a crown of thorns, placed it on his head. Then they began to salute him with, 'Hail, King of the Jews!' They beat him about the head with a cane and spat upon him, and then knelt and paid mock homage to him. When they had finished their mockery, they stripped him of the purple and dressed him in his own clothes.

'Then they took him out to crucify him. A man called Simon, from Cyrene, the father of Alexander and Rufus, was passing by on his way in from the country, and they pressed him into service to carry his cross. Jesus was offered drugged wine, but he would not take it. Then they fastened him to the cross. They divided his clothes among them, casting lots to decide what each should have.

'The hour of the crucifixion was nine in the morning, and the inscription giving the charge against him read, 'The King of the Jews.' Two bandits were crucified with him, one on his right and the other on his left.

'The passers-by hurled abuse at him: 'Aha!' they cried, wagging their heads, 'You would pull the temple down, would you, and build it in three days? Come down from the cross and save yourself!' So too the chief priests and the doctors of the law jested with one another: 'He saved others,' they said, 'but he cannot save himself. Let the Messiah, the King of Israel, come down now from the cross. If we see that, we shall believe.' Even those who were crucified with him taunted him.' ' Mark 15.16-32

For the soldiers it was a bit of fun. If this man was a king, dress him up and let's have a laugh. It was no more than that. Yet another crucifixion … rather boring! So they were to get the dice out and idle the time away until they could get back to barracks.

Why had Simon from Cyrene in North Africa given Jesus a helping hand with the cross? We do not know why. Maybe he was a follower of Jesus. Mark states that he was the father of Alexander and Rufus … an odd piece of information unless it was relevant. We don't know, but in Romans 16.13 Paul sends greetings to Rufus in the Church at Rome. Rufus would have heard the tale from his father and I like to think that Rufus was alongside Peter in Rome together with Mark as they recorded the events. Mark could not resist this personal

reference to Rufus's father. This was a second-hand witness account.

Golgotha was nicknamed the 'skull' because of its shape. It was the common place for crucifixions. The event of that day was almost too harrowing to write about. It was a fearful place.

'At midday, darkness fell over the whole land, which lasted till three in the afternoon; and at three Jesus cried aloud, 'Eli, Eli, lema sabachthani', which means, 'My God, my God, why hast thou forsaken me?' Some of the passers-by, on hearing this, said, 'Hark, he is calling Elijah.' A man came running with a sponge, soaked in sour wine, on the end of a cane, and held it to his lips. 'Let us see', he said, 'if Elijah is coming to take him down.' Then Jesus gave a loud cry and died. And the curtain of the temple was torn in two from top to bottom. And when the centurion who was standing opposite him saw how he died, he said, 'Truly this man was a son of God.' ' Mark 15.33-39

Matthew adds the story of an earthquake. Luke adds the saying 'Father into thy hands I commend my spirit'.

'My God, my God, why hast thou forsaken me?' are heart-searching words, but should be placed in context. They are part of Psalm 22 and Jesus would have known it by heart. Jesus on the cross might have been recalling the psalm … he probably had learnt it during his youth. It starts with this cry of despair, but the psalm moves on to a firm acceptance … 'All the ends of the earth shall remember and turn to the Lord; and all the families of the nations shall worship before him.' All was well. God will never abandon you. It is not a psalm which ends with sadness, but with wonder and glory.

The other Gospels use the phrase that it was 'finished'. The Greek word for 'finished' has overtones. The Greek pluperfect tense has a far deeper meaning than the English aorist tense. It means that what had to be done was 'utterly and completely finished, the task was done, it had truly been completed'. It was time for the last breath. The battle was over.

The symbolism of the torn curtain in the Temple is lost on us, but not to the Jews. The curtain concealed the inner sanctum, the Holy of Holies, where the high priest just once a year entered to plead with God on behalf of the nation. Mark suggests that the curtain was no longer needed. The miracle had been achieved. God was no longer contained in the Temple. The Temple was no longer needed. God is now in every person's heart. That was what the battle had been about. God never leaves you. There is no curtain between you and God. The work of Jesus had been completed ... it was finished.

An innocent man had taken all the evil that man could throw at him and, hand in hand with God, had seen it through to the end. Whatever this world throws at us, man cannot be destroyed. Evil is not going to win. That is a great message for each of us. The love of God will never fail you. In the end, we will not fail because love never comes to an end.

On the cross Jesus suffered as a man and it was as a human being that he achieved his victory. That victory was for us.

This is the crux of the crucifixion. There is nothing that man cannot face ... his God is always with him. Whatever happens in your life, your God is right there alongside you. Christ is truly our King and an example for us all.

Incidentally, the early Celtic church did not over-indulge in crosses although, of course, they existed. Those early Christians in Britain realised that Christ was King. That was the true Gospel. They had grasped the true meaning of the gospel. We are part of the Kingdom of God and Jesus is our King. He is our Majestas.

A Majestas had been placed on the outside west face of that sixth-century Cathedral in Llandaff, Cardiff and I am delighted that it is, after all these centuries, safely inside the building ... exceedingly tired and worn, but still a Majestas.

During my seven years of work and worship in that Cathedral, I

faced the Majestas every morning at half six and every evening going about my daily prayer. The question was asked every time … 'Is Christ your King?' It is a question not one of us can avoid. If your answer is negative, it is not too late. It is never too late, because God will never let you go and that is a guarantee. It was the message of Golgotha.

'He died for us and we must live for him' … now!

This was not really understood at first in the early church. They thought that there would be a 'second coming', that Jesus would return in glory. It is true that most texts infer that the second coming is not imminent, but the destruction of Jerusalem and temple after the Jewish revolt, AD 66-70, made the people think that the 'end' was near and Jesus would come to their rescue. They were still hooked on the hope of a political kingdom. They did not understand that the Kingdom of God had arrived already. Jesus had won his battle.

'In fact, the Kingdom of God is among you.' Luke 17.20

We rarely quote from the Gospel of Thomas. The question was … where is this Kingdom? The answer in the Gospel of Thomas was 'The Kingdom is within you and it is outside you'.

The Gospels reflect this thought. 'Search, and you will find; knock and the door will be opened'. Luke 11.19 That is Kingdom talk.

God's will for us is simple. Open your eyes. Look around you. When Jesus said 'Follow me', he meant 'Do it now!' The Kingdom is here about you. You are part of this Kingdom. Let us see the Love of God at work in you ... now! The only valid description of God in the New Testament is the phrase 'God is love'. We all have some understanding of the word love ... that is God at work inside you, whether you like it or not.

Mark at the beginning of his Gospel spells out the purpose of Jesus … 'The time is fulfilled and the Kingdom of God is at hand'. It was not about heaven, but about earth. It was not political. This is the 'good news' and it is for all of us.

Jesus, the man, endured all that this world could fling at him and survived in a spectacular way. There was nothing that could deflect the love of God that is in man. In truth he died to prove that we can all live in the Kingdom. His God never deserted him, but was with him every step of the way. The Kingdom of God is ours.

That is what Golgotha was all about.

Now it is time to explain the phrase ... 'he survived in a spectacular way'! We call it the resurrection.

Even his death has been questioned, but there should be no doubt that he died. We should now understand that God did not desert him and that the love of God is there for us all at all times. We live in his Kingdom and are not alone.

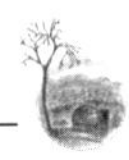

Chapter Four

THE REMOVAL OF THE STONE

Jesus was dead and entombed. Who moved the stone and was the tomb empty?
Was there a different resurrection body? Did Jesus rise from the dead?

Jesus was dead. He had been executed by the Roman soldiers by crucifixion, a death reserved for slaves and the basest of criminals. There was no honour in his death.

'taking the form of a slave…

And became obedient to the point of death –

Even death on a cross.' Philippians 2.7-8

And as far as the disciples were concerned, that was it. It was over. Jesus was dead. They had all failed him and gone into hiding. Peter had done his best, but even for him it was finished. All that was left was for a few women to bid farewell in their own way.

Jesus was dead. The normal Roman practice after a crucifixion was to leave the body hanging on the cross, to be picked at by the birds and animals. There were hundreds of such crosses on the Appian Way as you entered Rome. Human trash! They did not deserve burial. During the siege of Jerusalem in AD 69-70 there were thousands of Jews left to weather on their crosses. However, it was the normal Jewish custom to bury the body as soon as possible after the death.

We read that Joseph of Arimathea was brave enough to request the right to care for the body of Jesus. Even though Jesus was a 'criminal', they would have allowed this because Joseph of Arimathea was 'a respected member of the council, who was also himself looking for the Kingdom of God.' Mark 15.43

As far as Rome was concerned, Jesus was of little importance. The soldiers attending to the crucifixion were obviously ordered to supervise. Therefore it must have been the body of Jesus on the cross. After all, they had pierced his side with a sword to make sure that he was dead. They knew who it was and had enjoyed the fun they had over him and that is well documented.

Upon hearing of Jesus' death, this secret disciple of Jesus 'asked Pilate that he might take away the body of Jesus, and Pilate gave him permission.' John 19.38. Joseph of Arimathea immediately purchased a linen shroud Mark 15.46. and proceeded to Golgotha to take the body of Jesus down from the cross. There, according to John 19.39-40, Joseph and Nicodemus, another well known friend of Jesus, he then took the body and bound it in linen cloths with the spices that Nicodemus had bought. The disciples then conveyed the prepared corpse to a man-made cave hewn from rock in a garden of his house nearby. The Gospel of Matthew alone suggests that this was Joseph's own tomb. Matthew 27.60. The committal was undertaken speedily, 'for the Sabbath was drawing on'.

There appears to be no doubt that Jesus was dead and that his body was interred in a well-marked tomb.

It seems safe to accept that Jesus was buried in the way that the Gospels have stated. Joseph of Arimathea was an important citizen of Jerusalem, and that is why Pilate would have allowed him to arrange the burial ... not that it mattered much to Pilate. We can accept as fact that Mary Magdelene and Mary, the mother of Jesus, had checked where the grave was located. All that had to be done was done openly and legally.

'The women who had accompanied him from Galilee followed after; they took note of the tomb and observed how his body was laid. Then they went home and prepared spices and perfumes.' Luke 23.55

That was late on that Friday afternoon. Then came the Sabbath, Saturday. On the Sunday morning, early, 'Mary Magdalene, and Mary

the mother of James, and Salome, had brought sweet spices, that they might come and anoint him'. Mark 16.1

We all know what happened next ... or think that we do. The stone over the entry was already rolled back. Who moved the stone is a fair question? The absence of the body was too much for the mourners and the stage was set for the improbable to happen. There has been much written about who rolled the stone away.

'When the Sabbath was over, Mary Magdalene, Mary the mother of James, and Salome bought spices so that they might go to anoint Jesus' body. Very early on the first day of the week, just after sunrise, they were on their way to the tomb and they asked each other, 'Who will roll the stone away from the entrance of the tomb?'

'But when they looked up, they saw that the stone, which was very large, had been rolled away. As they entered the tomb, they saw a young man dressed in a white robe sitting on the right side, and they were alarmed.

'Don't be alarmed,' he said. 'You are looking for Jesus the Nazarene, who was crucified. He has risen! He is not here. See the place where they laid him. But go, tell his disciples and Peter, 'He is going ahead of you into Galilee. There you will see him, just as he told you.' Mark 16. 2-6

'There was a violent earthquake, for an angel of the Lord came down from heaven and, going to the tomb, rolled back the stone and sat on it.' ....Matthew 28 1,2

'But on the first day of the week, at early dawn, they came to the tomb, taking the spices that they had prepared. They found the stone rolled away from the tomb, but when they went in, they did not find the body. They were perplexed about this.' Luke 24 1-4

'Early on the first day of the week, while it was still dark, Mary Magdalene came to the tomb and saw that the stone had been removed from the tomb. So she ran and went to Simon Peter and the other disciple, the one whom Jesus loved, and said to them, 'They have taken the Lord out of the tomb, and we do not know where they have laid him." John 20 1-2

All accounts express the fear of the women, but Mark indicates the presence of a young man and then they all go on to talk about angels and earthquakes and the confusion and terror that overcame them. It must have seemed like a miracle. One can imagine the state of the women when they reported what had happened to the disciples. The tale would have grown in the telling.

Incidentally the Greek word for 'angel' is angelos which simply means a messenger. In one sense a mother caring for a child is an 'angel' conveying the love of God to her child. Peter was certainly present when the women returned with their peculiar message and this is what he asked Mark to write. It is the message from the young man whom they had met at the tomb.

I find it hard to believe that they could have persistently and successfully preached in Jerusalem a doctrine involving the vacancy of the tomb, without the grave being physically vacant. The facts were too recent and the tomb too close to the centre of Jerusalem

Incidentally, the empty tomb is not actually a proof of the resurrection. It is just an empty tomb. That is all that it is … an empty tomb. Another thought is that no-one considered a search for the body … if you questioned the resurrection that would have been the first thing to do. Rumours must have spread quickly that 'something' had happened. There would surely have been an 'inquiry' of some sort by the High Priests.

The most startling fact is that, after the death of Jesus, those disciples became followers and they made belief in the resurrection central to their faith. The eleven men were in hiding, totally disillusioned and disappointed. Yet, within a matter of weeks they were preaching the resurrection. Peter said 'God raised him from the dead, of that we are witnesses.' If that was not true, anyone could have

come forward and replied, 'That's nonsense; I can show you the body.' And all of this was within a mile or two from where the crucifixion had taken place. Take away the resurrection and you have little left. If there had not been the resurrection, Jesus would quickly have disappeared in history. It was the resurrection which transformed the disciples.

Paul's first letter to the Corinthians, chapter fifteen, is still read at most modern-day funerals. It is generally misunderstood. The Greek is translated into 'physical body' and 'spiritual body'. It sounds like two separate bodies. 'The bodies we now have are weak and can die. But they will be changed into bodies that are eternal.'

However, Paul's letter to the Romans 8. 9-11 rather contradicts this.

'If the Spirit of him who raised Jesus from the dead lives in you, he who raised Christ from the dead will give life to your mortal bodies also through his Spirit which dwells in you.'

That is very clear. There is no new body, but new life in your mortal body. Resurrection is the Spirit of Jesus in your present body. This is my 'new' body in the Kingdom of God. Does this mean that I have my resurrection body now? I think that is correct. My body remains the same, but the Spirit of God is in me … now.

Is this what happened to Jesus? I believe that there was no resurrection body ... it was the same body and Jesus goes out of his way to prove this.

All four Gospels seem just to tell a story with no explanation. They are reporting what was seen. They are eye-witness accounts. In fact there appears to be very little editing. Jesus is a mundane human being … he walks, he talks, and he eats fish. His body has remained the same. There is no transfiguration, no flashing lights, no stardom. Yet, he walks through doors and disappears and goes off to heaven. The writers record what they have seen with no questions or explanation.

The Gospels never suggest that we shall go to heaven (whatever that means today) when we die. They never say we shall be raised like Jesus. What they really say is that he is raised and a new world has begun and we are part of that world. In the end the disciples are told to go back to Jerusalem and await the Spirit of God. In fact they were at such a loss that they needed the Spirit of God to put life into them ... they needed this new life in their mortal bodies! After the resurrection came the Spirit which is the resurrection in us today. Our footsteps can be his footsteps. Jesus in us.

I believe that those disciples actually did meet a risen Lord I find no way of disbelieving that Jesus was raised from the dead, leaving an empty tomb, and was briefly seen by normal human beings and their lives were transformed. This transfiguration was in them! They certainly became 'new' men.

Most certainly if there had not been this remarkable happening; we would now know nothing about him. He would have been just another Jew killed off by the Roman soldiers. He might have earned a line or two as others have in some distant unimportant document, but no more than that. The pre-Easter Jesus would have died in the dust of Golgotha and been long forgotten.

But the tomb was empty. It would have been too easy at the time to prove that the tomb was not empty. The disciples had become a rabble and they had no will to arrange a conspiracy. In fact what happened was open and really public knowledge. The women talked, they all talked and they were all puzzled. It really did not make much sense. In fact it was all so puzzling that they could only talk about what had happened

And what did happen? Communicating any story is never easy ... we all select our own words and tell it in our own way. Let's go off on a slight tangent.

Carl Burke was a Chaplain in Erie County Jail in New York. His problem was how to communicate with the often hostile or indifferent youths from New York's toughest area. The world of West Side Story with no music and no glamour! Instead of trying to force the scriptures on these hard-to-teach youngsters, he encouraged them to retell the Bible stories in their own hip language. The only rule of the game was that they were to keep to the basic meaning of the Bible stories. He produced a book in 1966 entitled 'God is for Real, Man'. My copy is tattered and tired by usage. It certainly is not Shakespeare and will probably offend many purists, but just enjoy its spontaneity.

Touchin' Is Believin

After Jesus busted out of the grave

He met two of his gang on a road.

Man! Were they ever spooked and surprised.

They ran like crazy to the place where the other guys were.

And started to tell who they seen.

Before they could say much, bingo!

Jesus was there.

Came right through the door,

And they couldn't figure that out either.

He said, 'Peace!'

Good thing to say 'cause they was plenty scared

Knees shakin' and teeth jumpin'.

They thought for sure, this is a ghost.

And who wouldn't?

So Jesus says,

'What's buggin' you?

I ain't no ghost.

See, I got hands

And feet just like you guys.

Go ahead, touch me and see.

You know seein' is believing'

Well, they couldn't fight that; so they believed,

But, man, were they still surprised.

Just about then Jesus says,

'What cha got to eat? I'm hungry.'

So they gave him some fish fry.

After supper Jesus told them about how he busted

out of the grave

And why,

So that they could get rid of their sin and all

Of the bad things they did, and some did plenty.

The main reason for quoting that remarkable piece of writing is that I think that it contains a 'proof" of the resurrection. Read it again and see if you can spot it.

The writer has captured the surprise and shock of the disciples … 'knees shakin' and teeth jumpin' is surely a fair description of their mental trauma. Bingo! There he was and had come right through the door. It was a conversation stopper. There was only one thing that Jesus could possibly say at that juncture.

'Cool it!'

'Peace be with you.'

The reason that I am labouring the point is that it smacks of the truth. It sounds like an account of what actually happened. It sounds correct.

No-one wanted to believe in the resurrection.

As Luke said, they were 'startled and terrified'. Jesus showed them the wounds just to help them understand. This was no ghostly phantom of a body, but really was Jesus. Jesus in the flesh.

And if you were making this story up, there is no way that you would have made up the next bit.

'What cha got to eat? I'm hungry. And they gave him some fish fry.'

Luke adds 'and he took it and ate it as they watched.' Luke 24.43. This is surely an eye-witness account. The basic problem was that those disciples had given up. It was over and done with. There had to be something really dramatic to shake the disciples into belief. It required an atom bomb … we call it the resurrection. Nothing else would have done. Their 'knees were shakin' and teeth jumping'.

That helps me to understand and I accept the fact of the resurrection. The mechanics of what and how are beyond me, but it was the only way in which the defeated disciples could be animated and that they certainly were. There was no other way to put life into the apostles.

Not one disciple expected that there would be a resurrection and all doubted that it was real. Yet the accounts smack of reality and cannot be easily refuted. It took an atom bomb to convince his followers and it transformed them for life.

Chapter Five

RESURRECTION

TRUE OR FALSE

What did happen two thousand years ago?
Was it fantasy or reality?
There are many theories

Many theories have been advanced, attempting to show that the resurrection of Jesus Christ was a fraud. The theories, or alternate explanations, must take into account all the actions surrounding the resurrection of Christ. However, we can be agnostic and suspend judgement and that I suspect is the position of most of us. One must not force the evidence into a preconceived conclusion, but let all the evidence speak for itself. This study will cover only a few of the most popular explanations that have been set forth, generally by unbelievers or liberal theologians who attempt to explain away the resurrection of Jesus Christ. If you think the whole matter is absurd, you are entitled to that view.

You could say that the resurrection is not now vital to my belief and that it has done its work for mankind. Therefore the resurrection is not of much importance to me today, because as we shall see, we have moved on into the Age of the Spirit.

What was the purpose of the resurrection? It was simply to put new life into the disciples of Jesus. This was the only way for them and it worked.

Another purpose was to show mankind that nothing can separate us from the love of God and that we can be 'at one' with him ... we call it the 'atonement'. Jesus suffered the highest degradation that man

could face and he showed that the love of God will always prevail. We can win the world and good will always win against evil. The Kingdom of heaven is possible. The resurrection is nothing more now that an historical event. It achieved its purpose. With the spirit of Jesus in us we have faith that we shall succeed. We really have moved into the Age of the Spirit.

THE SWOON OR RESCUSCITATION THEORY

Jesus did not really die, he only swooned, so the disciples saw a revived or resuscitated Christ. Christ was nailed to a cross and suffered from shock, pain and loss of blood. But instead of actually dying, he only fainted from exhaustion. He was still alive and the disciples, mistaking him for dead, entombed him alive. After several hours, he revived in the coolness of the tomb, arose, moved the stone and then disappeared.

This theory completely ignores the evidence of his death and would require a greater miracle than the resurrection. According to this theory the cool damp air of the tomb healed him. He removed himself out of his garments which bound him tightly, had the strength to push the stone away, then eluded or fought off the guards, and shortly thereafter appeared before his disciples as the Lord of life. If in fact he had recovered from his wounds and lived beyond his thirty-three years, he then disappeared. Maybe he then lived with the disciples' incognito and they fabricate a story and were prepared to die for it.

'The next day, that is, after the day of Preparation, the chief priests and the Pharisees gathered before Pilate and said, 'Sir, we remember what that impostor said while he was still alive, 'After three days I will rise again.' Therefore command the tomb to be made secure until the third day; otherwise his disciples may go and steal him away, and tell the people, 'He has been raised from the dead, and the last deception would be worse than the first.' Pilate said to them, 'You have a guard of soldiers; go, make it as secure as you can.' So they went with the guard and made the tomb secure by sealing the stone.' Matthew 27 62-66.

'But Peter arose and ran to the tomb; stooping and looking in, he saw the linen wrappings only; and he went away to his home, marvelling at that which had happened.' Luke 24.12.

The Swoon Theory does not explain how the wrappings were undisturbed lying together, exactly as they had been when wrapped securely around the body of Christ. Christ would have had to perform a miracle of wriggling out of the wrappings which were, as was the custom, wound tightly about the body with over a hundred pounds of spices in the wrappings without someone to help unwrap him.

WAS JESUS DEAD?

If not, what condition would he have been in after the hours on the cross?

'The Jews therefore, because it was the day of preparation, so that the bodies should not remain on the cross on the Sabbath for that Sabbath was a high day, asked Pilate that their legs might be broken, and that they might be taken away. The soldiers therefore came, and broke the legs of the first man, and of the other man who was crucified with Him, but coming to Jesus, when they saw that He was already dead, they did not break His legs; but one of the soldiers pierced His side with a spear, and immediately there came out blood and water. And he who has seen has borne witness, and his witness is true; and he knows that he is telling the truth, so that you also may believe.' John 19.31-35

'Joseph of Arimathea came, a prominent member of the Council, who himself was waiting for the kingdom of God; and he gathered up courage and went in before Pilate, and asked for the body of Jesus. And Pilate wondered if He was dead by this time, and summoning the

centurion, he questioned him as to whether He was already dead. And ascertaining this from the centurion, he granted the body to Joseph.' Mark 15.43-45

He was dead in the judgment of the soldiers, in the judgment of Pilate, in the judgment of the Jews who requested the guard for the tomb, and in the judgment of the women who went to the tomb to further prepare the body by heaping spices over the body. 'The women who had come with Jesus from Galilee, followed Joseph and watched how Jesus' body was placed in the tomb.' Luke 23.5. Incidentally, the Roman soldiers had no interest in Jesus, he was of no importance to them and he would probably been put to death by them if the crucifixion had failed.

Even if Christ had only swooned, he still would have still been in a bad state after three long hours on the cross. A great deal of time would have been needed for recuperation. In His weakened condition ... beaten, crucified and stabbed ... he could not have walked the seven miles on the Emmaus road. It would have been unlikely for someone who had endured the beatings and crucifixion to so quickly give the impression that He was the Conqueror of death and the grave, and the Prince of Life

THE DISTORTION THEORY

This theory suggests that the original thoughts of the disciples were amplified and distorted as the legend of the resurrection of Jesus developed over the years.

This might account for the empty tomb, if you assume that the body was stolen, but fails to explain the sightings so soon after the event and the early claims of the disciples. Distortion can take many decades to evolve and cannot really be an instant phenomenon. The first statements of witnesses were graphic and the accounts were quite clear, but inexplicable to the witnesses.

Distortion requires time and thought, not instant reaction.

We accept that time will distort accounts, but the resurrection was an instant happening. Naturally everything grew in the telling and this we find has developed in the Christian Creeds over three hundred years.

THE HALLUCINATION THEORY

This theory says all of Christ's post-resurrection appearances were really only hallucinations. In this way, they can all be dismissed as figments of imagination.

How could so many people have similar hallucinations? Furthermore, the appearances happened under different conditions and were spread out over different times. And, do not forget, the disciples were reluctant to believe in the resurrection in the first place! This involves in all concerned a miracle of blindness ... hallucination ... to reason away the resurrection.

'When they heard that He was alive, and had been seen by her, it they refused to believe it. And after that, He appeared in a different form to two of them, while they were walking along on their way to the country. And they went away and reported it to the others, but they did not believe them either. And afterward He appeared to the eleven themselves as they were reclining at the table; and He reproached them for their unbelief and hardness of heart, because they had not believed those who had seen Him after He had risen.' Mark 16.11-16

'And these words appeared to them as nonsense, and they would not believe them.' Luke 24.11-12

'But Thomas, one of the twelve, called Didymus, was not with them when Jesus came. The other disciples therefore were saying to him, 'We have seen the Lord!' But he said to them, 'Unless I shall

see in His hands the imprint of the nails, and put my finger into the place of the nails, and put my hand into His side, I will not believe.' And after eight days again His disciples were inside, and Thomas with them. Jesus came, the doors having been shut, and stood in their midst, and said, 'Peace be with you'. Then He said to Thomas, 'Reach here your finger, and see My hands; and reach here your hand, and put it into My side; and be not unbelieving, but believing.' Thomas answered and said to Him, 'My Lord and my God!' Jesus said to him, 'Because you have seen Me, have you believed? Blessed are they who did not see, and yet believed.' John 20.24-30

Psychiatrists claim that only certain kinds of people have hallucinations. They are usually high-strung, highly imaginative, and very nervous. In fact, usually only paranoid or schizophrenic individuals have hallucinations. But Christ appeared to many different types of people. We read that he was seen by over five hundred at one time.

'He appeared to Cephas, that is, Peterand then to the Twelve. After that, he appeared to more than five hundred of the brothers and sisters at the same time, most of whom are still living'. 1 Corinthians 15.6

His appearances were not restricted to people of any particular psychological make-up. Hallucinations are linked in an individual's subconscious to his particular past experiences and this was certainly not possible with so many people. Hallucinations are usually restricted to when and where they occur, usually in a nostalgic atmosphere or in a place of familiar surroundings which places the person in a reminiscing mood. They occur in people when there is a spirit of anticipation or hopeful expectation. The historical record shows no such anticipation existed. They were prone to disbelieve even after they were told of the resurrection.

THE IMPERSONATION THEORY

This is the view that the appearances were not really Christ at all. But someone impersonating Him. The evidence for this is that in some cases they did not recognise him at first or at all'

The disciples were reluctant to believe in the resurrection, were doubtful and would have been hard to convince unless it was really him ... as was the case with Thomas.

It would have been impossible to impersonate Christ's wounds. This was Christ's proof to Thomas that it was really him. John.20 24

These men had travelled with the Lord for three years and it is incredible that anyone could have gotten away with an impersonation particularly due to their reluctance to believe.

Some meetings were in locked chambers when he suddenly appeared in his glorified body. No one could impersonate such a miraculous act other than the resurrected Christ.

THE SPIRITUAL RESURRECTION THEORY

This is the view that Christ's resurrection was not a real physical resurrection. Proponents of this theory assert that Christ's body remained in the grave and his real resurrection was spiritual in nature. It was only told this way to illustrate the resurrection such as might be our experience today. This is how we 'see' Christ today.

A physical body did disappear from the tomb. If it was only a spiritual resurrection, then what happened to the body? History shows there was a body there and it disappeared. The enemies of Christ were never able to produce the body, nor disprove the resurrection.

The resurrection accounts are not presented in parabolic or symbolic language, but as hard fact. John 20 is full of what Greek grammarians call vivid historical present tenses to stress the historical reality of the Gospel message.

The record states that he was touched and handled, that he had a body, and that he even ate with the disciples. Luke 24.30, 41f; Mark 16.12

THE THEFT THEORY

The disciples stole the body and then claimed that he rose from the dead. The chief priests tried to spread this rumour.

'Now while they were on their way, behold, some of the guard came into the city and reported to the chief priests all that had happened. And when they had assembled with the elders and counselled together, they gave a large sum of money to the soldiers, and said, 'You are to say, His disciples came by night and stole Him away while we were asleep. And if this should come to the governor's ears, we will win him over and keep you out of trouble.' And they took the money and did as they had been instructed; and this story was widely spread among the Jews, and is to this day. Matthew 28.11-15

Again, such a theory ignores the evidence of the linen wrappings and the empty tomb.

'and the face cloth, which had been on Jesus' head, not lying with the linen cloths but folded up in a place by itself. John 20. 7

If someone had stolen the body, they would have left the wrappings scattered or piled in a heap, but only resurrection could account for the position of the linen wrappings with the body absent. Who did it?

The Romans would not; they were there to guard it with their lives by Roman law and discipline. They had sealed the tomb and were there to prevent theft. The Romans had no motive to lose the body.

The women could not because they were worrying about the stone and how to move it. Mark 16. 3-4

The disciples were perplexed and scattered, huddled together in hidden rooms. Two had even left town, given up hope, and were on their way home to Emmaus.

The Jewish crowd would not and had actually requested a Roman guard to protect the tomb against theft. This is very significant because the presence of the Roman soldiers and the Roman seal over the door made the possibility of the religious leaders claims of theft a thousand times more difficult if not impossible. Mat. 27.63-66

The likelihood of these timid, scared Galilean disciples stealing the body of Jesus out from under the noses of a guard of highly disciplined and skilled Roman soldiers while they all slept (an offence punishable by death) is low.

THE UNKNOWN TOMB THEORY

One of the earliest theories present to explain everything away is that the disciples did not know where the tomb was located and could not have found the empty grave. This theory depends on the belief that those who were crucified were tossed into a common pit and were not allowed to be buried.

It disregards totally the straightforward historical narrative about the events surrounding Christ's burial and the post-resurrection scene. The Gospel record indicates that Joseph of Arimathea took the body to his own private tomb ... not a public mass-burial ground. According to Scripture, the body of Christ was prepared for burial according to the burial customs of the Jews; the women then sat opposite the tomb and watched. Not only did Joseph of Arimathea and the women know where the tomb was, so did the Romans ... they placed a guard there.

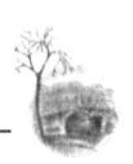

CONCLUSION

None of these theories ... and there are others ... adequately deal with the Scriptural facts that surrounded the resurrection of our Lord. The evidence says he rose from the dead and this resurrection for many Christians marks him out as the Son of God.

All the criteria stand up.

Of course we have doubts, but having faced them,
I believe that the resurrection is a fact.

I have no concept of how it worked, but still accept it.

Chapter Six

THE ASCENSION.

What happens next and what was the point of the resurrection? We encounter another puzzling happening and decide that we live in the Age of the Spirit

It had required a miracle to convince those disciples that he was alive. Surely they must have discussed this question ... 'What next?' Acts gives the answer and it is the beginning of a saga that stretches through time to each of us today. It is quite a story.

However, in spite of all that Jesus had said, many of the disciples still did not grasp what Jesus had taught them about the Kingdom. They still thought that the Kingdom was political. Acts tells it all. While the apostles were still with Jesus, they asked him, 'Lord are you now going to give Israel its own king again?' 'The answer was: 'You will receive power when the Holy Spirit comes upon you. And you will be my witnesses, telling people about me everywhere ... in Jerusalem, throughout Judea, in Samaria, and to the ends of the earth. After saying this, he was taken up into a cloud while they were watching, and they could no longer see him.' Acts 1. 6ff

'As He talked with His disciples, He told the apostles to wait in Jerusalem until they received power when the Holy Spirit came on them. Forty days after Jesus rose, he went back to be with God the Father. When he said this, as they watched, he was lifted up, and a cloud removed him from their sight.' Acts 1.9

We call it the Ascension of Jesus.

'He showed himself to these men after his death, and gave ample proof that he was alive: over a period of forty days he appeared to them and taught about the kingdom. You must stay in the city until you are given power from heaven.' Luke 24.49

Now they had their orders and the next 'happening' was what we call the Ascension. For disbelievers this will be more gobbledegook and miracle nonsense. It was the end of the resurrection. In a sense, the resurrection has little to do with our faith today. It was part of the process, albeit a vital part, in the creation of the Church and the fact that I am a Christian today and part of that process is the Ascension.

The trouble with the Ascension story is that involves antique cosmology. Flat earth, down below and up above, heaven up and hell down made sense two thousand years ago.

We have all long admired in art galleries the paintings of the Masters. Jesus on His way looking up to heaven, surrounded by angels and harpists in misty atmosphere with worshipping followers bidding Him farewell. How lovely! How beautiful! And as child I believed it.

And what is your picture? Did he take off like a rocket? First, he was two inches off the ground, then twelve inches and then shot up into the cloud. Where is he now? Is he still going and has he reached the edges of the Milky Way? Or maybe after the lift off, the launch was called off and he disappeared. Bingo … he's gone! That all really seems nonsense.

It was like a game … now you see him, now you don't and now he seems to have gone altogether. They only had words to describe what was happening and they did their best. Heaven and earth to them had nothing to do with location; they were places where God was at work. God was everywhere and that was the only way that they could describe it. He was 'down here' and 'up there' and if he was not 'down here', he had to be 'up there'.

The Ascension had little to do with time. Luke had a neat arrangement in his writing. Easter ... forty days later ... Ascension. Luke seems to be tidying up the events so that we can understand them. It was the start of the Christian calendar as we have it today. Forty was a magic number to the Jews. The Israelites when they escaped from Egypt were to spend forty years in the wilderness. Jesus after his baptism by John the Baptist spent forty days in the wilderness. Forty was considered to be the time that was needed to decide on anything to do with God ... at the end of that time God would act. So Luke has fitted the events into a time pattern.

The Ascension is really to do with Jesus and God and Jesus being 'let loose' into the whole world. He was released via heaven into the world. Words are difficult.

'Do you think that he is dead?'

'No, lady, he's not dead, but let loose into the whole world.'

John Masefield 'The Trial of Jesus.'

Christ is our King and rules over us. 'God has exalted him and given him a name which is above every name; that at the name of Jesus every knee should bow, of things in heaven, and things on earth, and things under the earth.' Philippians 2.10-11

The Ascension asserts the sovereignty of Jesus Christ. They explained it as best they could. The order given them by Jesus was to stay in Jerusalem and wait.

'Then they returned to Jerusalem from the hill called Olivet, which is near Jerusalem, no further than a Sabbath day's journey. Entering the city they went to the room upstairs where they were lodging: Peter and John and James and Andrew, Philip and Thomas, Bartholomew and Matthew, James the son of Alphaeus and Simon the Zealot, and Judas the son of James. All these were constantly at prayer together, and with them a group of women, including Mary, the mother of Jesus, and his brothers.' Acts 1. 12-14

The whole 'gang ' was there, still puzzled and excited. What next?

'While the day of Pentecost was running its course they were all together in one place, when suddenly there came from the sky a noise

like a strong driving wind, which filled the whole house where they were sitting … and they were all filled with the Holy Spirit.' Acts 2 1

The Ascension story is all about the coming of the Holy Spirit.

Some years fifty years ago, I was in the bar at Kingston House … the headquarters of the Mersey Mission to Seamen in the heart of Liverpool … and I was clutching a 'Padre's Special'. Don't get excited, that was a half tankard of an inch of Watneys Red Barrel topped up with lemonade … no wonder my teeth fell out! Alongside me was a seafarer who had just come in from Portland on the east coast of America. His name has long gone. I have no memory of how the subject emerged in our casual chat, but out of the blue I recall his question.

'What's all this talk about the Holy Spirit?'

That put me on the spot as I had to give an answer that he could understand. Happily, I remembered what I had been taught in Sunday School as a child by a coalminer called Reg Hutchins.

'The Holy Spirit is the little bit of God inside me.'

My seafaring companion was quiet for moment and then faced me with another poser.

'Are you telling me that all Christians have a little bit of God inside them?'

'Yes, I am. It's rather crude language, but I really believe that all Christians and all of humanity, whether they like it or not, have a little bit of God inside them.'

The pause was even longer and then he made a statement which I regard as one of the most perceptive statements that I have ever heard.

'In that case, if that is true, we should be able to see him!'

When Paul wrote to the folk in Galatia he was saying the same thing. If you really have the Holy Spirit, it should show in your life. How can you judge that the Spirit of Jesus is in you? Paul said that the answer is simple, the harvest will be obvious to all and here it is.

'The harvest of the Spirit is love, joy, peace, patience, kindness, goodness, fidelity, gentleness and self-control.' Galatians 5 22-2

If Jesus taught me anything, I'll settle for that lot. In fact I believe that most of us have all those qualities, but there is still a problem … it's almost impossible to have them all at the same time. But please note the first gift of the Spirit is love. Read that list again and I am certain that you will agree that, as an agenda for those who would be in the Kingdom of God, the list is perfect. This is the way that mankind should be living together. It is our Highway Code.

Cranmer and his Book of Common Prayer have much to answer for. He endlessly uses the phrase Holy Ghost ... not Holy Spirit. It troubled me as a child as I imagined God arriving in a white bed-sheet and making banshee noises.

Eventually, as I grew up, the word 'ghost' was dropped in churches and 'spirit' replaced it. Incidentally, I still meet pious folk who think that we have debased the language in our churches as they are convinced that Jesus spoke in a seventeen century lingo. The fact that it was all originally written in Greek and well-spiced with Aramaic is ignored.

The Spirit of Jesus is in us and demands our obedience and trust. The Spirit of God is part of our life. We all have gifts and Paul put it this way; The Spirit works in believers, through the gifts given us by God. All these are inspired by one and the same Spirit, who apportions to each one individually as he wills. 1 Cor. 12.11 Through the Spirit the love of God is poured into hearts. Romans 5.5 Through the Spirit the Christian has been transplanted into the freedom of sonship. Gal. 4.6 The personal centre of all our lives is the Holy Spirit. The Holy Spirit is 'the little bit of God inside you'.

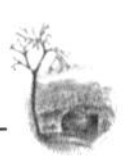

Is it the same when I learn to 'love God and my neighbour'? Why not? It is a love affair and it should show in your life. You are learning to share your life with Jesus and to look at life as Jesus saw it. You are meant to see the world through the eyes of Jesus. It means that there is nothing secular in this world, because everything contributes to the building of the Kingdom of God. You see God at work everywhere. You really are looking at the world with the eyes of Jesus. That is love. We should be working hand in hand with him so that the Kingdom is here on earth and we are part of it. This is our love affair. You are meant to look at the world through his eyes

'I would like to rise very high, Lord

Above my city

Above the world

Above all time

I would like to purify my glance and borrow your eyes.'

I have no idea who wrote that but to 'borrow' the eyes of Jesus makes sense to me. It would be the end of war and conflict, of hate and sorrow, the end of pain and suffering … or would it? In fact we would see the pain and suffering much clearer and surely that would make us strive to put an end to war and hate. The eyes of Jesus are not rose-tinted, but twenty-twenty. We are blind. We have to see the hate and the sorrow in order to replace them with love. In the midst of all the anguish of mankind, we must see the love of God there with us at all times. We must travel hand in hand.

If we knew how to look at life through the eyes of God, we should see the God of love seeking the love of his creatures. We are meant not to walk with lowered eyes, but to search for Him through things, events and people. Everything should reveal the presence of God to us. Long prayers are not needed in order to smile at Christ at work in the smallest detail of daily life.

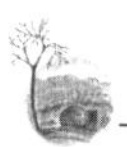

The Spirit of Jesus is with all of us if we only look.

New life was given to the disciples and the result is that we all live today in the Age of the Spirit.

Chapter Seven

LOVE AND THE SPIRIT

What is the resurrection all about? 1 Corinthians 13 is the crux of the whole of Jesus' life. A good look at the word 'love'. What is 'agape' all about and how can you possibly love your enemies?

What was the real point of the Resurrection and the life of Jesus? The disciples certainly missed the point and this made the resurrection necessary ... but even this was not entirely successful. They still thought like Jews because they were Jews. In this sense the resurrection failed. As we shall see, there had to another resurrection appearance for Paul and that did work. If the first resurrection failed, the second succeeded.

Think about Jesus and the point of his life. What was his message to the world. We read that it turned the world upside down. Basically his teaching was very simple and most people know what it is. He asked us to do two things.

Love God ... the 'good' ... and love your neighbour.

Love is the heart of our religion and if it is not there, we are getting it wrong. Religion without love is man-made and not a religion. That is the message of Jesus. All other faiths must have this criterion if they are of value to mankind. A religion which does not home in on love is suspect.

This word 'love' is rather a basic concept. If I were placed on a desert island and only allowed one chapter of the bible, there would be no difficulty in choosing.

'I may speak in the tongues of men or angels, but if I am without love, I am a sounding gong or a clanging cymbal. I may have the gift of prophecy, and know every hidden truth; I may have faith strong enough to move mountains; but if I have no love, I am nothing. I may dole out all I possess, or even give my body to be burnt, but if I have no love, I am none the better. Love is patient, love is kind and envies no-one. Love is never boastful, nor conceited, nor rude; never selfish, not quick to take offence. Love keeps no score of wrongs; does not gloat over other men's sins, but delights in the truth. There is nothing love cannot face; there is no limit to its faith, its hope, and its endurance.

'Love will never come to an end. Are there prophets? Their work will be over. Are there tongues of ecstasy? They will cease. Is there knowledge? It will vanish away; for our knowledge and our prophecy alike are partial, and the partial vanishes when wholeness comes. When I was a child, my speech, my outlook, and my thoughts were all childish. When I grew up, I had finished with childish things. Now we see only puzzling reflections in a mirror, but then we shall see face to face. My knowledge now is partial; then it will be whole, like God's knowledge of me. In a word, there are three things that last forever: faith, hope, and love; but the greatest of them all is love.'

I suggest that this is the most vital passage in the whole of scripture and, in fact, the theme is present in most of the great religions of the world. The conviction of the importance of this passage came very early in my life and that truly was a blessing because it has taken me ninety-five years to work out the full implication of these thought-words ... and I am still at it. Love is what it is all about and it is not easy. Most of us misunderstand the word.

I keep repeating that the only understandable description of God we have is 'God is love'. As every person has some knowledge of love, it follows that each one of us has a 'little bit of God' inside him whether he likes it or not. God is in all of us.

The study of this chapter ... 1 Corinthians 13 ... has over time enabled me to live happily with most of the ecclesiastical baggage which I have acquired in my lifetime from my Church. However, I cannot stress the importance of carrying that baggage because in it

there will be ultimate truth. Freely I acknowledge that without the Church, the early hours of prayer on cold winter mornings, the pain of sharing so much suffering with people and the barren periods of my pilgrimage through life, there would not have been a better vehicle which could have carried me across the nine decades and, to change the metaphor, that very Church has proved to be the sounding board to test what has, at last, become the ultimate thought. That thought is so simple that I hesitate to voice it yet again ... 'if there is no love, there is nothing'. And the prime source as I have journeyed to uncover that apparently simple truth has always been Jesus.

Paul is the person to give us help, not only because he has left us a vast amount of writing on matters spiritual, which have withstood some two-thousand years without being discredited, but Paul also has the advantage of basing his writings on the personal contact he enjoyed with those who had personal contact with Jesus. Whilst we cannot uncover the 'ipsissima verba', the very words of Jesus, Paul does reflect their influence. If you feel the need to go 'back to basics', Paul is as good as any person to take you there.

'Without love, you are nothing.'

Religions of all kinds and sorts carry far too much baggage, collected over the centuries and this circumference of religion is too often confused for its centre. The baggage has produced almost unbelievable, unwise and sub-human controversy. The soul, the centre, of religion is love.

Let's look again at this soul-word. Love is not just passion. Often there is no tenderness to be found in passion. Love is not just good nature ... and yet that is part of it. Love is not natural kindness. That can so often disappear at a whim. Am I saying that love is unnatural? Look at that thought.

It is easier for the strong to care (I have used a lesser word than 'love' just to make these points) for the weak. That can almost be natural. But, it is really hard for the weak to care for the strong and is almost asking too much.

It is easier for the rich to care for the poor than for the poor to care for the rich.

It is easier for the beautiful to care for the ugly, but possibly really tough for the ugly to care for the beautiful, let alone love them!

We could continue these examples. If the word God troubles you, make it 'the highest good' you can think of and beyond that. Thus when we are exhorted to 'love God', the relationship that we have with God is that of us being weak, poor and ugly, etc., and we should not be surprised that it is difficult. We are obviously lesser than God. Put simply, loving God is not a natural activity of man. How can it be? Of course, the truth is that the concept of God is truly beyond us.

I can only cope with the idea that I can find God in the image of Jesus. That is an important statement. The word 'God' has little meaning for me although I am fairly steeped in the intricate thoughts of theology and have spent a life in the search. Remember John 1.18.

'No one has ever seen God. The only Son ... has shown us what God is like.'

We have Jesus and I can find and understand the meaning of love by meditating (that is only a 'posh' word for 'thinking') on the life of Jesus. The Jesus figure makes all my understanding of God possible and, almost as a by-product, the meaning of that word love.

Maybe the better way of dealing with 1 Corinthians 13 would have been to start at the end. Many murder mysteries make more sense if you have the courage to do just that.

'There are three things that last forever: faith, hope, and love; but the greatest of them all is love.'

I am uncertain about the use of the word 'faith', so let's look at it. This whole chapter actually rests on faith. Faith is almost a primitive thing and is an instinct. It is not reason and therefore cannot

be broken by reason. It actually seems to be unreasonable. Faith on its own is unsound. It needs the next step, which is in the word 'hope'. I suspect that Paul uses this final sentence to indicate that we should have faith in Christ and then also have the hope that we can put our future into the hands of Christ and that this is the basis of love. There is no preparation in the text for these thoughts. Whilst faith has been mentioned in v.8 'I may have faith strong enough to move mountains' 'hope' arrives from nowhere as it has not been spoken of until the final verse. I hope that my faith is sound!

Incidentally, we all depend upon faith every moment of our lives. For example we have faith that the milkman has not poisoned our milk and that the bus driver has passed his test!

Greek was the superb language of the time and remains today as unrivalled in expressing shades of meaning. Examine the Greek word for love. Paul uses agape and I will return to it. There are other Greek words for love.

eros (erotic, etc.) This is the word for love between the sexes. It does not appear in the New Testament.

storge This is to do with family affection or love for your nation.

philia (philosophy, love of knowledge, etc.) This is the commonest word in the New Testament for love. It is a great word, friendship, the love of a husband and wife. The best English translation is 'cherish' which is used in the 1662 Book of Common Prayer as part of the marriage vows. It expresses warmth.

In this chapter the word love in Greek is agape and is an odd choice at first glance. The word is used in variant forms 250 times in the Bible and the problem is 'Why abandon the other Greek words for love?' The other words were probably regarded as unsuitable. eros had certainly been debased by usage with over-tones of passion. storge was too narrowly associated with family. philia was restricted to the near and dear, a lovely word but not wide enough. So that leaves agape, ... 'brotherly love' ... a word rarely used in Classical Greek, but adopted in a big way by Paul.

Christian love (agape) must certainly extend to the nearest and dearest, but must go further, to friends, to fellow Christians, to the neighbour, to the enemy, to the entire world. In other words, agape has to do with the mind … and not the heart. It is not an emotion which comes over us; it is a principle by which we deliberately live. No-one naturally loves an enemy. To do that you must conquer your emotions and natural inclinations and even your reason. This is the power which enables us to love the unlovable, to love the strong, the rich, and the beautiful. It is an attitude of mind!

So what is the meaning of agape? The supreme passage explaining it is in Matthew.

'You have learned that they were told, 'Love your neighbour, hate your enemy.' But what I tell you is this: Love your enemies, and pray for your persecutors; only so can you be children ... sons ... of your heavenly Father, who makes his sun rise on good and bad alike, and sends rain on the honest and dishonest. If you love only those who love you, what reward can you expect? Surely the tax-gatherers do as much as that. And if you greet only your brothers, what is extraordinary about that? Even the heathen do as much. You must therefore be all goodness, just as your heavenly Father is all good'. Matthew 5.43-48.

I note that Jesus asks us to think of goodness when we think of God. My phrase is 'goodness and beyond that' and that is my vague concept of God.

We are told to love our enemies. Why? The answer is astounding. In order that we should be sons of God. Me a son of God? The explanation goes on. God sends his rain on the just and the unjust and on the evil and on the good. This spells out so clearly that no matter what a man is like, God seeks nothing but man's highest good.

That is agape. It is an attitude of the mind.

No wonder Paul starts the next chapter with a simple command. 'Put love first.'

Let me just add what might be the next thought. There is no way that I can grasp this agape stuff on my own. I need help' with my attitude of mind. That help is available to us all. The help available to us is, of course, the Spirit of God ... or the Spirit of Jesus.

And that is another story which brings the Spirit of Jesus right down to us today. This is what the resurrection is all about. The purpose of our faith is to bring love to all mankind ... and that really is a challenge. The resurrection was all about love and you and all mankind.

Grasp the meaning of 'agape' and you will understand the difficulty and joy of trying to follow the Master.

Chapter Eight

THE RESURRECTION ACCOUNTS

Was Jesus different from the rest of mankind? How did we decide that he was divine?
We look at the Stilling of the Storm and how the story grew.
The Gospels were influenced by Judaism, yet can be trusted.

Whilst the resurrection was vital to the survival of what was to become Christianity, it probably was not regarded in the early years as important. The first century Jews were expecting the rising to life of all righteous dead to herald the coming of their kingdom when God would return in glory and restore Israel to its ultimate dream. Resurrection was part of the 'dream' in Judaism. However, the rising of one man, though striking in itself, was not sufficient to move the Jews into expectation of the coming of their saviour ... the Messiah ... and incidentally that basically is their understanding today. He is yet to come. The Jews would have been unmoved by the resurrection of Jesus ... a man crucified with two others would not have been of much account, regardless of the stories of his appearances. He died the death of a criminal. This means that there must have been other motivations to lead to the ultimate title bestowed upon him ... the Son of God. Jesus must have been different.

If Jesus had been a disreputable character, a rogue, philanderer or drunkard, the outcome of the apparent return to life would have been simply laughable. If he had been just a teacher of moral tales, a good man, the resurrection would have been regarded as just a sad end to such a man, just a sad curtailment of a life. It certainly would have not moved the world! They expected more of the Messiah.

Maybe, Jesus did qualify as different in his teaching, maybe his talk about Kingdom was for real. Certainly this eventually was the way that the disciples began to understand the words of Jesus. They

had misunderstood the meaning of words 'kingdom of God' because after all they were Jews and their misunderstanding was naturally Jewish-based on their idea of an earthly kingdom. The resurrection surely had been necessary to correct the thoughts of those disciples. It was not easy to change the Jewish kingdom thoughts to Kingdom of Heaven thinking, but that is why the resurrection was important and necessary.

A major problem was Jesus himself. He was certainly different and did remarkable things which the disciples found hard to understand. They were naturally confused and this coloured their memories and the way in which they recorded his story. Was Jesus a man or a divine being became the question. By the time that the Gospels were written, some three or four decades after his life, Jesus was being seen as the Son of God and his humanity was fading. This fact is clearly evident in how his life was rewritten ... the 'stilling of the storm' is a good example of this. It was edited to prove his divinity.

It had been a long, hard day, teaching and talking endlessly to the crowds who had thronged him. He was tired and hot and in need of rest. The only way that he could escape the crowds was to board a fishing vessel and pull away from the shore. It is recorded in Matthew 8 23-27, Mark 4.45-41, Luke 8:22-25

'That day when evening came, he said to his disciples, 'Let us go over to the other side.' Leaving the crowd behind, they took him along, just as he was, in the boat. There were also other boats with him. A furious squall came up, and the waves broke over the boat, so that it was nearly swamped. Jesus was in the stern, sleeping on a cushion. The disciples woke him and said to him, 'Teacher, don't you care if we drown?' He got up, rebuked the wind and said to the waves, 'Quiet! Be still!' Then the wind died down and it was completely calm. He said to his disciples, 'Why are you so afraid? Do you still have no faith?' They were terrified and asked each other, 'Who is this? Even the wind and the waves obey him!' Mark 4.35-41

How this story ends up in that written form is interesting. It gives Jesus power over land and sea and for those early Christians that makes him some sort of a divine being. So maybe the prime question is what really happened on that boat. Did he still that storm? If he did, what relevance is that to me today?

I recall discussing this tale with seafarers aboard a ship in Liverpool. It was a small Irish coaster which faced almost every week in winter a full gale with waves over the top of the bridge. Those men knew about storms. To my surprise they disagreed about the message in the Gospels. They said that these were fishermen well used to the sudden squalls, quite normal on the sea of Galilee, but probably this particular blow had caught them by surprise and there was real danger and possibly a bit of panic. And there was Jesus fast asleep ... 'Wake up we're in trouble here! Don't you care!' The response of Jesus was natural ... 'Cool it lads! You know what to do! Get on with it! I'm trying to sleep here.' The squall passed as quickly as it had arisen and all was well. This made a lot of sense to me. All that was required was to deal with the potential panic and surely that was what Jesus did. It was important to control the fear in the men. We all need help in the storms of our lives. Those seafarers to whom I was listening knew that the task of Jesus was to 'still' those men ... the storm was incidental.

Then in that cabin we talked about Jesus. These men in front of me knew all about the dangers of the sea. Surely it was more important to quieten the fishermen than the storm. This is what Jesus can do for us to help us in the storms of life. That was the real point of the story. That made much more sense to them and to me than some miracle with wind and wave.

Yet we are stuck with the Gospel account. The main message in the story is that Jesus' disciples should have faith in God who looks over you and cares and stills the storm. The Gospel writers were answering the question, 'Who is Jesus?' The tale had grown in the

telling, like Chinese whispers. The disciples began seeing Jesus as divine and the Son of God with power over all things, on land and sea.

The need to prove the divinity of Jesus slowly influenced their memories and coloured all the writings that we have. The humanity of Jesus was quietly being lost. This can be seen in many of the stories about Jesus and is totally understandable.

Next we recall that for the Jews all history had to be 'according to the scriptures'. It was important that the works of Jesus had been foretold in scripture ... if he really was the Son of God. Psalm 107, verses 23 to 32 are perfect in showing how this 'stilling of the storm' story was adapted to conform with 'according to the scriptures'.

The opening verses of the psalm talk about YHWH (God) saving those whom he has redeemed. It talks about God's people going on the sea in ships to do business. God 'commanded and raised up the stormy wind' ... Ps 107.25 ... and the sailors were scared (26-27). However, when they cried out to YHWH, 'he brought them out from their distress' (28) by stilling the storm. They were then glad and praised Him (30-31).

This is so similar to the story of Mark that we can take it that Mark was conforming to this. We can read 'they cried to YHWH in their trouble' (28) as being changed to the similar disciples' cry to Jesus in Mark 4:38, but there is a difference in the ending. In the psalm, the saved sailors give thanks to God whereas in Mark's account they are rebuked for having no faith. Mark writes εφοβηθησαν φοβον μεγαν ('they were filled with a great fear') which probably means the fear of YHWH rather than being scared of the dangerous storm.

We can also note that much of the story of stilling the storm is very similar to that found in the opening chapter of Jonah. The connection between the two stories may not seem particularly obvious. God causes a fierce storm to blow up (Jonah 1.4, Mark 4.37), which panics the sailors (Jonah 1.6, Mark 4.37). This causes them to accuse the main person of dereliction of duty because they were fast asleep

(Jonah 1.6, Mark 4.38). In both cases, only God can stop the storm (Jonah 1.15, Mark 4.39) and because of this the chorus of sailors is awestruck (Jonah 1.16, Mark 4.41). Jesus is greater than Jonah, for in Jonah's case he had to be thrown overboard (Jonah 1.15) so that God might stop the storm, whereas in Jesus' case, he merely needs to talk sternly to the storm.

The Gospel writers were trying to retell the resurrection story as an Israel story. It was not enough to say that this man had risen from the dead. It had to be part of Jewish history. Never forget that for the Jews their 'today' history had to be 'according to the scriptures'. Proof texts were needed to back this sentiment. The teachers in the early church did the same. The resurrection of Jesus had to be seen as the work of God.

The 'first' church in Jerusalem was entirely composed of Jews, including the apostles. They practised Judaism, meeting in the Temple and in local synagogues.

Paul, a Jew, was aware of the Jesus stories and we read that he spent at least a fortnight with Peter in Jerusalem when, he met some of those who had lived with Jesus and who had witnessed the first resurrection. It is clear that Paul was also listening to their thoughts about Jesus.

'For what I received I passed on to you is of first importance: that Christ died for our sins according to the Scriptures, that he was buried, that he was raised on the third day, and that he appeared to Cephas (Peter) and then to the Twelve. After that, he appeared to more than five hundred of the brothers and sisters at the same time, most of whom are still living, though some have fallen asleep. Then he appeared to James, then to all the apostles, and last of all he appeared to me also, as to one abnormally born.' 1 Corinthians 15.3-8

The Jerusalem group must have collected stories about Jesus and his teaching. This oral testimony was eventually to be recorded and becomes the Gospel writings. Again, we must remember that the

Gospels were 'worked over' so that they accorded to scripture and this would have been done in good faith. Also we must remember that 'his' story was also used as a teaching manual and would have been remembered and written in this way. A story is told and then the moral is explained ... this is the nature of teaching.

Part of the 'fun' in studying the Gospels is to uncover the editing of many decades. It might be called quasi-biography and is actually the way in which all of history of mankind is recorded. Every happening in historical writing is coloured by the author and is naturally subjective.

The Jesus story is really a Jewish story and is acknowledged as such ... 'according to the scriptures'. A complication is that the stories were not only told in the Jewish world but in the Gentile world and that meant that they had to be presented as biography to people who knew nothing of the Jewish background. How far the life of Jesus was edited to fit in with both the Jewish and the Gentile approach to history is obviously debateable. It all adds to the 'fun'. And this particular problem was the task of one man ... Paul, for whom 'resurrection' was a reality and for whom the world was to become almost entirely Gentile-orientated.

Paul revealed next to nothing about the life of Jesus in his writing and it is as though the human Jesus did not exist. Resurrection to him was the appearance of Jesus to him on the Damascus road.

'We are careful not to judge people by what they seem to be, though we once judged Christ in this way. So if anyone is in Christ ... he is a new person! The old has passed away; see, it has become new.' 2 Corinthians 16-17

Paul surely is saying that he knew personally nothing about the human Jesus, but goes further to say that such knowledge is irrelevant. He really is acknowledging that the 'according to the scripture' approach from the apostles is irrelevant as far as the Gentiles are concerned. Forget about the past. And this makes sense. He never speaks about the works and miracles of Jesus. He is concerned about the 'new' Jesus that he found in his resurrection experience.

'I have become a slave to everyone, so that I can win as many people as possible. When I am with Jews, I live like a Jew to win Jews. They are ruled by the law of Moses, and I am not. In fact I am ruled by the law of Christ'. 1 Corinthians 9.20ff

Paul's teaching centred on understanding the death and resurrection of Jesus Christ as a turning point in history. He understood the resurrection to signal the end of the need to live under Jewish law. Instead Paul taught of living in the Spirit in which the power of God was made to work through human flesh. Some of his letters to fledgling churches throughout the Roman Empire are contained in the New Testament and outline Paul's theology. He insisted that Gentiles had as much access to the faith as Jews and that freedom from the Law set everyone free. It was this teaching which was essential for the development and success of the early church which would otherwise have remained nothing more than another Jewish sect.

Papias, AD 70, who was the Bishop of Hierapolis ... modern western Turkey ... claimed that Mark penned his gospel in Rome as Peter's scribe and makes this statement.

'Mark, having become the interpreter of Peter, wrote down accurately, though not indeed in order, whatsoever he remembered of the things said or done by Christ.'

Justin Martyr, AD 103, Clement of Alexandria AD 150 and many others all backed the claim of Papias.

Peter is mentioned twenty-six times in Mark's, gospel compared with Matthew who names Peter only three times in his much longer gospel. Remember that Matthew includes and copies almost every written word of Mark so he adds very little to the story.

Mark shows much respect to Peter compared with the other

writers. In the account of Jesus walking on water ... Matthew 14.22-33 ... Peter sadly fails to copy this, he is called a man 'of little faith'. Mark omits the whole incident. In the account of the miraculous catching of fish ... Luke 5.1-11 ... Peter tells Jesus to 'Go away from me Lord, for I am a sinful man'. Mark omits the whole incident. When Peter makes a rash statement like saying that Jesus would not die ... Matthew 16.21-23 ... the least embarrassing response of Jesus is in Mark. Again and again, Mark uses a kinder expression when referring to Peter.

There are many more examples which could be quoted, but it cannot be denied that in Mark we have the definite thoughts of Peter who must be regarded as a reliable witness. All of the arguments implies that the witness accounts of the resurrection in the Bible can be trusted.

The disciples were puzzled by their life with Jesus of some three years and did not grasp the purpose of his life which was to establish the Kingdom of God on earth.

The Gospels were biased by the need to be 'according to the scriptures'.

The influence of Peter' writing through Mark is vital to the story.

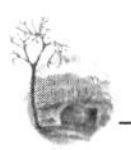

Chapter Nine

THE SECOND RESURRECTION

The early 'church' evolved and got it wrong and the Christians suffered. Paul emerges as an important figure as a result of the Second Resurrection on the road to Damascus. The 'church' is divided, but survives under Paul guidance.

What happened after the Resurrection? The real question might be how did the faith evolve after Golgotha. How did Christianity begin and does it all make sense. What was the effect of the Resurrection?

The 'coming of the Spirit' is well written up in the Acts of the Apostles and it became the impelling force that held those early followers together as they worked out the implication of the life, death and resurrection of Jesus. At first they were a dejected and a defeated group until the unexpected happened. Jesus had to shake them out of despair and give them hope. Even after the appearances there was no plan, just a desire to remember and relive the life which had given them strength. They were disorganised and had no sense of purpose or direction. Jesus had to tell the disciples to gather in Jerusalem and wait for the Spirit and that is what they did.

The Jews were completely at ease with the language about the 'divine spirit'. For them it would be the beginning of the 'great age' when they were to come into their Kingdom which was controlled by the Spirit of God. Thus this concept was embraced by the followers of Christ as a natural happening. Slowly over many decades they developed the concept of the Holy Spirit. They became the new family of Christ ... let us call it 'the early church'. They still carried on with two acts of Jewish discipline because they were Jews. Baptism and the Eucharist were part of their Jewish life and had to be reinterpreted by the new church.

Baptism was naturally regarded as the entry into this new sect. They all had heard Jesus talk about his baptism by his cousin John and realised that it had been vital to the start of his ministry. Baptism in Judaism is for spiritual cleansing and its use in Christian worship was continued as an entry into Christianity, such as it is today.

In the same way the Eucharist ... taking bread and wine on the eve of the Sabbath ... was part of the history of Judaism, recalling the delivery from Egypt. This was the Red Sea happening, the Mount Sinai and the Ten Commandment episode, the beginning of the new life in Israel. It would be taken for granted that this was to remain as part of their way of life. Over time, the concept was changed by Christians and it became accepted as a weekly celebration of the resurrection of Jesus ... this was the new life in the Kingdom. So the Eucharist ... in remembrance of Christ and not the Jewish Passover ... was associated with the death and rising again of Christ. Now we celebrate Easter Day every Sunday. Eucharist means 'thanksgiving'.

So the followers of Jesus incorporated Baptism and the Eucharist as part of their adoration of Jesus and this became the centre of their daily prayer lives.

The Romans persecuted this early movement from its early days because to them they were atheists who paid no homage to Nero, the emperor. Rome accepted and tolerated the stance of Judaism, but began to have doubts about this new off-shoot. People informed Rome of the presence of Christians, claiming that they were subverting the life of the community. The early Christians were at risk and not accepted by Rome or by the Jewish aristocracy.

There are non-Christian writers who give us some idea of the approach to Christianity in its formative years.

Tacitus, a Roman historian, writes in his Annals, following a fire in Rome in AD 64. He wanted to blame the Christians as the originators.

'Nero fabricated scapegoats and punished with every refinement the notoriously depraved Christians (as they were popularly called). Their originator, Christ, had been executed in Tiberius's reign by the governor of Judaea, Pontius Pilatus. But in spite of this temporary setback the deadly superstition had broken out afresh. They were dressed in wild animal skins to be torn to piece by dogs, or crucified or made into torches'.

Josephus, another Roman historian, adds to the story by writing about what was happening in Jerusalem, where a Christian 'church' (a Greek word ecklesia which means 'an assembly') had developed and, even though it was strictly for Jews and not Gentiles, the power of Judaism was pitted against it.

'They brought together a man named James, the brother of Jesus, who was called the Christ, and others ... and delivered them to be stoned.'

This was the background behind Paul's emergence as a Christian and he was active as a Christian in the early fifties. He was certainly involved in Corinth and Ephesus and we have his writings as evidence. It was a dangerous time to be a Christian and he suffered for his faith, especially after the fire in Rome in AD 64.

Saint Paul is undoubtedly one of the most important figures in the history of the Western world. Just a quick look at the headlines of his life are enough to understand his impact; his works are some of the earliest Christian documents that we have, 13 of the 27 books of the New Testament are written by him, and he is the hero of another ... Acts of the Apostles. He travelled thousands of miles around the Mediterranean spreading the word of Jesus and it was Paul who came up with the doctrines that would turn Christianity from a small sect of Judaism into a worldwide faith that was open to all.

What we know about Paul, first known as Saul, comes from two extraordinary sources. The first is the Acts of the Apostles, written after Paul's death, almost certainly by the same author who wrote St

Luke's gospel. There is evidence that Acts was written to pass on the Christian message, but behind the theology lie clues about Paul's life. The author of Acts claims that he knew Paul and even accompanied him on many of his journeys. The second source is Paul's own letters. They represent Paul's version of events, and it seems reasonable to accept them as the more reliable account of his life.

Saul was born in Tarsus (now in the south east of Turkey) to a Jewish family. He had a dual identity as lots of Jews did in antiquity; Saul was both a Jew and a Roman citizen. He had a Jewish education, a Jewish way of life and abided by the Law of Moses, but was brought up outside the homeland, fluent in Greek, and he understood and embraced both the Greek and Roman cultural traditions.

He was a Pharisee, one of a group of Jews who policed the boundary of the Mosaic law. His task was to make sure that they and others were faithful to the law of Moses. Saul was an extremely passionate Jew and he often uses the word 'zeal' of himself. The most important story about Saul is his incredible transformation on the Damascus road, but one thing that did not change in this transformation was his passion. He just becomes passionate for a different cause.

Saul of Tarsus first appears in the biblical record as a witness to the stoning of Stephen, the first martyr to the cause of Christ ... even 'consenting' to his death. Acts 7:58; 9:1 Henceforth his persecution of Christians, as portrayed in the book of Acts via his own testimony, was relentless, though he thought sincerely he was doing Jehovah's will. 23:1; 26:9 Pursuing the saints even unto foreign cities...26:11... he beat, imprisoned, and had them put to death. 22:19 Later he would write that 'beyond measure I persecuted the church of God, and made havoc of it'. Galatians 1:13

Here was a man who had devoted his life to debunking the early followers of Jesus ... that was his calling. 'Let's put a stop to this nonsense here and now' was the main purpose of Saul's life.

'The church in Jerusalem suffered terribly. All the Lord's followers, except the apostles, were scattered everywhere in Judea and Samaria. Saul started making trouble for the church. He went from house to house, arresting men and women and putting them in jail.' Acts 8.3

But Saul was stopped in his tracks. Jesus appeared before him … nothing else would have worked. As a result he was a changed man … he was transfigured. His message now was ... 'I have seen the Lord!' This is what I call 'the second resurrection'

Saul was the complete Jew ... strict observance of the Torah, the laws of being a Jew, prayer and fasting, and above all, a fierce and loyal devotion to the God of Israel. Yet a few years later he would write of glimpsing 'the glory of God in the face of Jesus the Messiah'. His conversion was all about Jesus. The Temple and all that it had stood for was now over and the new reality for him was that all of Judaism had led to the coming of Jesus.

And this was a few years after the Easter appearances in Jerusalem. The date must have been about AD 36. Paul calls his experience the 'appearance'. It was no dream, no ghost, no vision … he met Jesus on the road to Damascus and as a result he became the most important apostle of all.

'When Saul had almost reached Damascus, a bright light from heaven suddenly flashed around him. He fell to the ground and heard a voice that said 'Saul! Saul! Why are you so cruel to me?'

'Who are you?' Saul asked.

'I am Jesus,' the Lord answered. 'I am the one you are so cruel to. Now get up and go into the city, where you will be told what to do.'

'The men with Saul stood there speechless. They had heard the voice, but they had not seen anyone. Saul got up from the ground, and when he had opened his eyes, he could not see a thing. Someone then

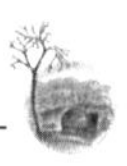

led him by hand to Damascus and for three days he was blind and did not eat or drink.' Acts 9 3-9

Sometime later Paul gives us firm details about what happened next after his experience on the Damascus Paul was shocked and stunned and blind for three days. His world was upside down. The words 'God' and 'Israel' had taken on a challenging different meaning. Fifteen years later he wrote these words 'There is no longer Jew or Greek; there is no longer slave or free; there is no male or female, you are all one in the Messiah Jesus.' This is where the road to Damascus led Paul. It turned him into a 'Messiah man', but above all Paul received the spirit of Jesus. Jesus was alive in him. Paul was special because of his knowledge of the scriptures and he was well placed to put Jesus into the history of Israel and into the world.

'I went away to Arabia, and then returned once more to Damascus. Then three years later I went up to Jerusalem to become acquainted with Cephas (Peter), and stayed with him fifteen days. But I did not see any other of the apostles except James, the Lord's brother.' Galatians 1.15-19

One wonders whether in Arabia he found himself at Mount Sinai, which is a 'place of beginnings'. I, too, have been there and felt the presence of history. It is full of Moses where he received the Torah, it is where Elijah went when all was going wrong and it was where Saul of Tarsus found his strength to announce the new King of Mankind.

I call the road to Damascus the Second Resurrection.

This happening was vital for the emergence of the 'Christian church' and the fact that it was open to all people, not just the Jews, enabled it to become world-wide within a few years. This was the great break-through.

As we have seen Paul in time travelled to Jerusalem where he was eventually accepted by the apostles and was instructed in the basics of Christianity. There he stayed with Peter for two weeks and presumably learned much more about Jesus from him. . Here he also met Barnabas. The oral tradition must stem from that Jerusalem 'church', but Saul makes little of it in his writing. We must assume that the gospels were not written by this time ... all was oral.

Surprisingly, Paul then disappears for a period ... roughly AD 36-46 ... and worked as a tent-maker with his sleeves rolled up and chatting to his customers about his experiences. Tarsus was his hometown and he had returned to his family and friends. It was a time for prayer and meditation and fitting his Jesus into his knowledge of Judaism. There was much to think about.

Everything culminates with Jesus. Whilst Judaism homed in on the Torah and the Temple, Paul was now centred on Jesus, who was the Messiah ... the new Messiah for all mankind and not just for the Jews. This was the new message ... Jesus is King. He is our Majestas. Above all, this was not in the future, but now. The new Kingdom is here and for us all today. We have no clue as to how Saul arrived at this conclusion. We do not know whether there was a Jesus community in Tarsus, but he must have discussed his thoughts with others and surely built up a following. The breaking of bread together would have helped to create a body of worshippers. His zealous enthusiasm for his newly-found Jesus must have been infectious.

It took time to move from Judaism to a 'faith-for-all' which enabled all humans to be set free to worship God. There was to be no barrier in this new faith, but this would have been difficult for his family and friends. Happily, Saul, understood the power of love which became one of his strongest of messages, but being estranged from his fellow Jews and possibly family would have caused deep hurt.

At the end of Saul's ten years, the 'church' in Jerusalem was facing a problem concerning Antioch. Apparently a division between Jews and Gentiles was creating a difficulty. The faith was obviously divisive, but there were other questions. What about business

partnerships, friendships and inter-marriage, even the food you ate, the Jewish 'day-off' for the Sabbath and the general questions about 'them and us'? It was necessary to send an envoy to Antioch. This was the third biggest city in the Roman empire and became the centre of the movement to expand this new Christian sect ... the sect of Jesus the Nazarene.

Barnabas was sent to see what was going on there. He, like Saul, believed that Jesus was the man for all people and deserved loyalty and allegiance, which was exactly what Caesar demanded of his own subjects. The Greek word is pistis which means total commitment to the God revealed in Jesus. We might call it 'faith'. It was a completely new way of approaching life. Barnabas remembered the contact with Saul when so many years previously he had visited Jerusalem for just fifteen days and felt that he was the man to help him in Antioch. They remained for a year and there for the first time the followers were called Christianoi ... a Greek word which was almost a joke; the oily ones, the anointed ones, the Messiah freaks ... the new King. And it stuck! The good folk of Antioch wanted to send money to help the Jerusalem church and in AD 47 Barnabas and Saul did just that.

They shocked Jerusalem with their fervour for Jew and non-Jew being one family and it became one of Saul's main themes. The gift of money was symbolic of being one family ... one koinonia ... a word meaning 'friendship', wanting all us to be ecumenical ... a Greek word which means basically 'in one house together' ... friends, one family in Christ, not Catholic and Protestant ... one in Christ! They had also taken Titus with them, a non-Jew, a firm believer, and the Jerusalem sect were enraged ... they did not approve of Titus. They could not eat at the same table unless Titus was circumcised and claimed that this was essential for him to become a full Christian. James, Peter and John finally agreed and the problem was resolved. Titus was accepted. Saul and the two friends returned to Antioch. This time they took with them a young colleague called Mark, who was a special friend of Peter and related to Barnabas.

Saul and Barnabas were next chosen to go to Cyprus where Barnabas had family connections. This was 47-48 There they went from city to city, often meeting hostility but sometimes a welcome. Generally, they started in the local synagogues and Saul was the main speaker. Cyprus is quite small and word would have travelled about the three itinerants and their message. There he changed his name to Paul. I suspect that the name Saul had too many overtones about his past activities.

How did Paul build the followers into what he began to call 'churches' and then emphasised the need for unity and holiness in these small bodies? He sees these new groups as firmly linked into the history of Judaism, going back to Abraham and links the new movement with this history. It was a fresh concept and out of it came a different kind of human society. The poor and vulnerable, the slave and ethnic minorities, suddenly found a 'togetherness'. It was a vast improvement on the pagan world which surrounded them and left them drifting. They were creating a caring society for all people and this was a new approach for society. One group gave financial help to another ... there was a collection to help the poor in Jerusalem. 'Shine like lights in the world' was a theme which led to 'good works' for others. Those early Christians were doing things which did change and enhance society. Paul was long gone by the time that Christianity led the caring world into a further concept of society ... education and medicine. Sadly these thoughts often led to abuse and cruelty and total misunderstanding, but the vision has remained and is with us today. This is our Kingdom and Jesus is our King. The deep roots of all of this can be traced back to Paul and his clarity of thought has never faltered. Basically, he had the vision of one God reshaped around Jesus and the Spirit and this was the framework of his world. We are meant to be a caring world.

Leaving Cyprus, they sailed to Pamphylia and Mark, who had joined them, returned to Jerusalem where he undoubtedly reported on the work achieved and probably was not well received. Next they

moved on to Galatia.

The message was that Jesus was the new Messiah, fulfilling the scriptures of Judaism from Abraham to David and all the prophets and that this message was even for non-Jews. This was the breakthrough. The Messiah was now the Lord of all the known world. This was the new Kingdom for all. Paul was revealing a Jesus who was part of the divine plan of God for mankind and it was a separation with Judaism.

Jerusalem was the natural centre for the Jesus movement with the presence of James, the brother of Jesus, as the leader. The other two pillars there were Peter and John. They still orientated to Judaism and saw the Messiah as the leader to bring freedom for the Jews. This stance led to conflict with Rome and the ultimate destruction of Jerusalem in AD 70.

The Jerusalem group naturally centred on the Temple and the Torah. 'Torah' has a range of meanings. It can most specifically mean the first five books of the twenty-four books of the Tanakh, and was usually printed with rabbinic commentaries. Incidentally, the Hebrew Bible, also called the Tanakh, is the canonical collection of Jewish texts, which is also a textual source for the Christian Old Testament. It can mean the continued narrative from the Book of Genesis to the end of the Tanakh, and it can mean the totality of Jewish teaching, culture and practice, whether derived from biblical texts or later rabbinic writings. Common to all these meanings, the Torah consists of the origin of Jewish people; their call into being by God. These texts are composed mainly in Biblical Hebrew, with some passages in Biblical Aramaic. The traditional Hebrew text is known as the Masoretic Text. Tanakh is an acronym of the first Hebrew letter of each of the Masoretic Text's three traditional subdivisions: Torah, Nevi'im and Ketuvim.

Paul and Barnabas were suspect because it looked as if they were saying that they no longer needed the law of Moses and the Torah. There was no longer need for circumcision. Paul's converts, the non-

Jews, were therefore not expected to accept the Judaist rules and thus were also under suspicion

About AD 48-49 Paul was called back to Jerusalem to account for his activity. It proved to be an important visit, but there are different accounts of what happened. However, he never mentions it in his writings. It seems that there was a very strong movement outside Jerusalem to convert the non-Jews to Judaism. This was the great divide amongst the followers of Jesus ... the need to convert Gentiles (non-Jews) into Jews. After all, following Christ was a Jewish movement; he was a Jewish Messiah. There was a hard-line party which insisted on the Torah and circumcision, but to Paul's surprise Peter was unconvinced and accepted Paul. The crisis was averted.

Paul believed that the Gentiles were alive with the new life of forgiveness, acceptance and transformation, and that they didn't need to be circumcised. So he brought this idea to the leaders in Jerusalem and when the Jerusalem council reluctantly agreed that Gentiles could become Christians without becoming Jews first, there was much relief. This was a momentous decision. Jesus and not Judaism was the basis of faith.

'I have been nailed to the cross with Jesus and I no longer live, but Jesus lives in me. The life I now live in the body, I live by faith in the Son of God. Galatians 2.20

You can get some idea of Paul's passion when you read the letter to the Galatians. A group of his converts had decided that they wanted to be circumcised and Paul was absolutely furious about this because he felt it compromised their very nature as Christians. You can almost feel him banging on the table or pacing round the room as he dictated the letter. At one stage right towards the end of the letter he grabs the pen out of the scribe's hand and he says 'see with what large letters I am writing in my own hand'. He is really frustrated. Paul never shied away from conflict.

Paul was a tough man. He could take all kinds of controversy

and suffering. He has, in one or two of his letters, long lists of the things that he has endured. He writes about the number of times he has been beaten, the number of times he's been put in prison, the number of shipwrecks he's endured and he seems proud of them. He was physically quite weak, but he always attributed his staying power to the grace (help) of God or the power of God. He had a strong sense of experiencing the power of God through suffering.

'I have worked harder, been put in prison more often, been whipped times without number, and faced death again and again. Five different times the Jewish leaders gave me thirty-nine lashes. Three times I was beaten with rods. Once I was stoned. Three times I was shipwrecked. Once I spent a whole night and a day adrift at sea. I have travelled on many long journeys. I have faced danger from rivers and from robbers. I have faced danger from my own people, the Jews, as well as from the Gentiles. I have faced danger in the cities, in the deserts, and on the seas. And I have faced danger from men who claim to be believers but are not. I have worked hard and long, enduring many sleepless nights. I have been hungry and thirsty and have often gone without food. I have shivered in the cold, without enough clothing to keep me warm. Then, besides all this, I have the daily burden of my concern for all the churches.' 2 Corinthians 11.23ff

Paul was a great writer. He wrote what was probably an early Christian hymn. Wonderful words!

'Let your bearing towards one another arise out of your life in Christ Jesus. For the divine nature was his from the first; yet he did not think to snatch equality with God, but made himself nothing, assuming the nature of a slave. Bearing the human likeness, revealed in human shape, he humbled himself, and in obedience accepted even death ... death on a cross. Therefore God raised him to the heights and bestowed on him the name above all names, that at the name of Jesus every knee should bow ... in heaven, on earth, and in the depths ... and every name confess, 'Jesus Christ is Lord', to the glory of God the Father.' Philippians 2. 5-11

'Jesus Christ is Lord' was the first Christian Creed and I feel that it is all that you need to understand the basis of Christianity and to call yourself Christian. Jesus Christ is Lord. Later in his letter to the Philippians, Paul describes his life before he met Jesus as mere garbage … a better translation is actually 'dung'! Paul concludes, 'All I care for is to know Christ.'

As an aside, I recall a conversation with the late Bishop Stuart Blanch, the Bishop of Liverpool, later the Archbishop of York, in which we were chatting about commitment. After a silence, he said this. 'If I had to be martyred for my Christian belief, I could write it on a postage stamp what I might be prepared to die for and the word bishop or church would not appear. All that is necessary is the simple statement that 'Jesus Christ is Lord'. Paul would certainly agree with that.

Paul never mentions the empty tomb, because for him Jesus was alive in him and all those resurrection stories were not important. It was all done and dusted, but he never forgot his own experience.

Much has obviously been written about Paul and the early church ... all relevant and important, but the most vital of all is the place of Paul in history. Was Paul the founder of Christianity such as we have today? Christ may be the corner stone of the church, but was the real architect Paul?

Starting from 30 AD, the writings in the New Testament are fundamental to understanding the early Church and the importance of the resurrection.

Our first real contact with the resurrection is the story of the Road to Emmaus. The disciples had given up on Jesus. His life had ended on the Cross and whilst they had listened to his teaching they had not understood. The Kingdom of Heaven to them meant the return of power to Israel and the end of Roman domination.

That generation of first century Jews were expecting the raising to life of all the righteous dead as part of the moment when domination over the Romans came. The news that only one man had appeared to have risen from the dead meant that nothing had changed and, though it was 'news', it had little effect upon their future hopes. His resurrection ... one assumes that they were fully aware of the stories ... had little meaning in the world of Judaism.

For the resurrection of Jesus to produce results much more was needed to be known about the man and that surely was the task for the disciples and the purpose of the Gospels. They had to 'sell' Jesus to the world. Mark starts his Gospel with simple words ... 'This is the Gospel ... meaning 'good news' about Jesus Christ.' It was not enough that a man had risen from the dead, it was necessary to prove it from the scriptures. Judaism saw their history as the means of transforming the way in which the tale was told. Nothing else would have been acceptable. Because of this the Gospels are not just a biographical outline. The telling of the Jesus saga had to define how Jesus was fulfilling the history of Israel and. as we have discovered, this meant re-writing history.

Without Paul there would have been little to write about. Paul's writings are the closest in time to the resurrection days. Here was a man who devoted his life to debunking the early followers of Jesus … that was his calling. But Paul was stopped in his tracks. Jesus appeared for him … nothing else would have worked. There had to be another resurrection appearance. As this was exactly what had been needed for the disciples, so it was for Paul. He was a changed man … he was transfigured. His message now was, 'I have seen the Lord!' And this was a few years after the earlier Easter appearances … the word that he uses is 'appearance'. It was no dream, no ghost, no vision … he knew that he had met Jesus on the road to Damascus. The Second Resurrection proved to be the real foundation stone for Christianity.

In his letters, we discover the Paul who writes warmly to his friends, both men and women, the Paul who frets about how the members of his churches are coping without him and who defends their status as true converts and we even find the Paul who appeals for the freedom of a slave. But like all great and charismatic figures there is another side. The Paul who berates his followers for back-sliding and doubting, the Paul who tells women to keep silent and condemns homosexuality, and the Paul who stood up to Peter, one of the most senior people in the early church.

Academics are trying to piece together these scraps of information with a new technique that is rather like a combination of sociology and forensic anthropology they have come up with a picture of Paul who would be a man of his time and place, a hot-headed Mediterranean who would be quick to defend his honour and the honour of his followers and who would demand loyalty in return.

Paul wrote some of the most beautiful and important passages in the whole bible, but his works have also been used, amongst other things, to justify homophobia, slavery and anti-Semitism. He is also accused of being anti-feminist, although many modern scholars would argue that in fact that he championed the cause of women church leaders. In the final analysis, Paul was the first great Christian theologian, establishing some of the building blocks of faith that we now take for granted, though there are those who argue that in laying his ground rules, he has obscured and separated us from the true teachings of Jesus. But perhaps the true sign of Paul's importance is that even nearly 2,000 years after his death, he still inspires passion. Whatever you feel, it is hard to be neutral about Paul.

Our Christianity was moulded by him and as a result of Paul's resurrection experience we have our Church as it is today

That second resurrection was vital.

Paul was the architect of the modern church and had to win the clash between
the Jerusalem church and the Gentile church.

We must not underestimate the importance of Paul.

Paul's ministry set the church in motion around the world. Christianity was different

and brought a new light to mankind.

The message was 'Jesus Christ is Lord'.

Chapter Ten

THE RESURRECTION AND ME

We consider the value of imagination and the Spirit of Jesus in us. Then we evaluate the importance of knowing Jesus, and finally we decide who Jesus is and the place of love in our lives.

My dear old mother has long gone, probably is only remembered by me now and I am past ninety-five. But I can still hear her voice ... and I mean hear ... 'Robert!' Whenever I heard those strident tones, I knew that I was guilty as charged. On the odd occasions when all was well, I was addressed as Bob. But it goes much further than that. In a real sense I can converse with her today, sixty years later. Of course, I cannot touch her or see her, but I know what she would have me do. In other words, she is as alive for me today as ever. She is still there for me. Imagination? Who cares? It is a helpful form of life after death.

My wife died nineteen years back. I had sat behind her at school at the age of eight. We knew each other! For me today she is not dead, but still alive. If there is life after death, this is it! As long as I live, she will never die. That is what love can do for you because love can never die. There is no need for her to come through doors for me to touch her. Her spirit is fully alive in me. I cannot explain this. Her body was tired and worn-out and could not continue. Her spirit is still vibrant. Explain it as you may, we still walk hand in hand because love never dies. Her spirit is alive in me today. This really is much more than imagination. Again, I feel that this is positive life after death. Imagination? If you think not, I cannot argue because you have a right to your opinion.

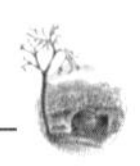

Is that what we mean when we talk about the Spirit of God? Incidentally, the word 'God' means little to me. But all is not lost.

'No-one has ever seen God.

The only Son, who is truly God and is closest to the Father,

has shown us what God is like.' John 1.18.

If my only knowledge of God's activity is in what I know about Jesus, it is enough for me. I want Jesus alive in me today Surely this is the resurrection. I have thought about him, studied his life and ceaselessly talked about him. Jesus is alive in me today. The resurrection for me is about today, not two thousand years ago.

Bishop Tom Wright of Durham wrote this:

'Indeed, precisely because part of that new possibility is for human beings themselves to be revived and renewed, the resurrection of Jesus does not leave us passive, helpless spectators to go and make new creation happen in the world.'

That is the nub of the matter. It was as though Jesus at last got those disciples by the scruff of the neck, shook them and told them to get on with it. It was time for action. And that they did. That is what the resurrection did for them, just as it can do for me. This allows me to walk day by day with Jesus holding my hand. The resurrection is about today and is not lost in history.

People might say that this is all in the imagination. They are quite right. I agree. Of course it is in my imagination! Where else could it be? That does not make it unreal. I can imagine Rhossili Bay in the Gower Peninsula and that is reality. I can imagine my children, Stephen and Jane and Martin, who is sadly no longer with us, and they are real to me and I do not need to be with them physically to feel at one with them. Their spirits are alive to me all the time.

Imagination and reality always end together in your mind. When I look at Rhossili Bay, it registers on my mind and it yet is more than what I can see ... like a dream I find memories of past happiness which transform what I actually am looking at into much more than sight.

This surely is what Martin Luther King Jr. (1963) in his famous speech saw was the future for mankind. His dream was far greater than imagination.

'I still have a dream, a dream deeply rooted in the American dream ... one day this nation will rise up and live up to its creed. We hold these truths to be self evident: that all men are created equal. I have a dream...'

Thank you John Lennon for that beautiful song 'Imagine'.

You may say that I'm a dreamer

But I'm not the only one

I hope someday you'll join us

And the world will be as one

You cannot prove 'love', but you can live it, feel it, breathe it and base your whole life and being on it. If you have not yet experienced the strength of love, this thought is difficult for you. Trust, faith, understanding are exactly the same and without them, you are not really living. Surely all of this is imagination but is real. This, said John Lennon, is the real world. Join it.

I seem to recall that I have read much about the Greek word pneuma, which is the word 'spirit'. Incidentally, you all use that Greek word almost daily … pneumatic tyres … you pump air into the tubes otherwise you are flat! This is the new breath and it is the breath of Jesus. No wonder they talked about the coming of the spirit like a wind sweeping them off their feet … 'a strong driving wind, which filled the whole house where they were sitting.' Acts 2.2. How else could they describe it? It swept them off their feet. Love can do this.

I believe that the resurrection of Jesus and the spirit of Jesus is a today-happening, giving life to me today. I only have today ...

yesterday is gone and tomorrow is not here. The Spirit of Jesus must be a 'now' happening. Of what real use to me is a story of what happened two thousand years ago in a back-water of a country! It is the spirit of Jesus today that enables me to walk in his footsteps. This is love in action.

Jesus knew about love and he knew that one of his disciples was badly scarred after all that had happened on Golgotha. I am very fond of Simon Peter because most of us are like him … we never quite get it right. Think about Peter … it is like looking in a mirror.

Simon Peter, at the beginning, was not called to follow Jesus; he just turned up with his brother out of curiosity. Incidentally, your new life could start the same way. Just turn up and talk and listen. That is all that he did. Andrew was also Simon's brother and brought him along. Jesus gave Simon a remarkable greeting. Jesus 'looked him in the face, and said, 'You are Simon, son of John. You shall be called Cephas' ' ... that translates into 'Peter' ...petros ... the Greek word for a rock. Rock-man was a most unsuitable name for Simon as he was at that time.

Peter became a disciple, but carried on with his fishing until Jesus finally called him. 'Come after me, and I will make you to become fishers of men.' Mark 1.17 Being a disciple was no sinecure. Jesus became involved again and again in difficult discussions in many synagogues and as a result we read that 'many of the disciples withdrew and walked no more with him.' His mission was failing. Jesus turned to the inner Twelve and asked 'Do you also want to leave me?' Peter spoke up for them and rallied the disciples … 'Lord, to whom shall we go? Your words are words of eternal life. We have faith.'

But, by this time, little was going the way Jesus had hoped. His mission was failing badly. He had been rejected by his own family; the people of Galilee had shown their displeasure and the religious leaders viewed him with suspicion. They misinterpreted his miracles.

The main trouble about a miracle is that it is like a conjuring trick, if you missed it, you say, 'Hey, Lord, do it again.' And there is no way that I would follow Jesus because he turned water into wine. Distilleries are good at that. And what difference does it make to me that Jesus might have stilled a storm? Miracles prove nothing! That was why Jesus told folk 'Do not tell anyone what has happened'. He healed the sick out of compassion, not to make a name for himself.

So they arrived at Caesarea Philippi. It was to be an important crossroad in the life of Jesus. Jesus felt that he was losing his disciples and he had to confront them. If you recall, Jesus took Peter, James and John apart and put to them the question ... 'Who do men say I am?'

'Jesus and his disciples set out for the villages of Caesarea Philippi. On the way he asked his disciples, 'Who do men say I am?' They answered, 'Some say John the Baptist, others Elijah, others one of the prophets.' 'And you,' he asked, 'who do you say I am?' Peter replied: 'You are the Messiah.' Then he gave them strict orders not to tell anyone about him; and he began to teach them that the Son of Man had to undergo great sufferings, and to be rejected by the elders, chief priests, and doctors of the law; to be put to death, and to rise again three days afterwards. He spoke about it plainly. At this Peter took him by the arm and began to rebuke him. But Jesus turned round, and, looking at his disciples, rebuked Peter. 'Away with you, Satan,' he said, 'you think as men think, not as God thinks.' ' Mark 8.27-33

Pause a moment. 'You are the Messiah.' Messiah and Christ mean the same ... the King. These are important words. The word 'Christ' is derived from the word which means 'to anoint'. It occurs many times in the Old Testament and is connected with the anointing of the Kings of Israel ... part of the coronation ceremonial as it is in our coronation ceremonies in Westminster Abbey. Peter was calling Jesus the Messiah, the King, the anointed one. The other disciples had the same idea about him being a King because James and John were

to approach Jesus a little later and ask, 'Grant us the right to sit in state with you, one at the right and the other at your left.' Jesus realised that they still did not understand and thought he would be an earthly king. He had to tell them again that he would be killed. That did not go down very well. It was not the Messiah that they were expecting.

It is possible that this was the first time that those disciples saw a new depth in Jesus ... a new glory, to use a New Testament word. They never doubted that Jesus was truly and fully a man, but now they began to sense that maybe God was in this man. However, they were not entirely convinced because they knew his humanity ... he was a man ... and it was only subsequently, some decades after the resurrection that they all began to believe in the complete divinity of Jesus.

There was another title that caused confusion … 'the Son of Man'. Actually it is probably just an Aramaic expression for a man, a human being. I am a son of man. He really was saying that he was a human being; you can see me and touch me. Jesus was to rebuke Peter for attempting to glorify him … 'Begone, Satan. You shall do homage to the Lord your God and worship him alone.' Those were tough words for Jesus to use against Peter. Peter got it wrong many times and was firmly corrected by Jesus. Jesus did not think himself divine!

Caesarea Philippi was the Rubicon in the life of Jesus. It was almost a relief. The confusion of the wanderings in Galilee and the following mobs were now over. Ahead lay Jerusalem and the final climax of his life. He realised that he had to take his disciples by the hand and lead them every step of the way. It was not going to be easy for him and at the very last minute he was to hesitate and pray that this cup should pass from him.

Then came the occasion of feet-washing … quite a story.

'When it was Simon Peter's turn, Peter said to him, 'You, Lord, washing my feet?' Jesus replied, 'You do not understand now what I am doing, but one day you will.' Peter said, 'I will never let you wash my feet.' 'If I do not wash you,' Jesus replied. 'you are not in fellowship with me.' 'Then, Lord,' said Simon Peter, 'not my feet only; wash my hands and head as well!' John 13.8-9

Dear old Peter went in well over the top and got it wrong again, but that was the kind of person he was. And next came the denial episode … he denied all knowledge of Jesus three times. We know why he had to deny his contact with Jesus ... it had taken much courage to be near Jesus at the end ... but it left Peter totally shattered.

What was Jesus to do to restore Peter?

'This makes the third time that Jesus appeared to his disciples after his resurrection from the dead. After breakfast, Jesus said to Simon Peter, 'Simon son of John, do you love me more than all else?' 'Yes, Lord,' he answered, 'you know that I love you.' 'Then feed my lambs', he said. A second time he asked, 'Simon, son of John, do you love me?' 'Yes, Lord, you know I love you.' 'Then tend my sheep.' A third time he said, 'Simon son of John, do you love me?' Peter was hurt that he asked him a third time, 'Do you love me?' 'Lord', he said, 'you know everything; you know I love you.' Jesus said, 'Feed my sheep.' ' John 21.15-17

In the end, the answer was simple. 'You know Lord, that I love you.' It was enough. The question was posed three times possibly to remove Peter's guilt of denying Jesus three times. All was well. It was a love that brought Peter eventually to a cross. He asked to be crucified head downwards for he said that he was not worthy to die as his Lord had died.

Possibly Peter, when he dictated his memories for Mark to record, was not as spiritually minded as John was in his Gospel. Possibly he did not take the good news to the ends of the earth as did Paul, but one thing Peter did superbly well. He knew how to follow the footsteps of his Lord. He could walk hand in hand with Jesus. It was enough.

The Jesus who had asked Peter if he loved him is now asking the civilised world to respond to the same question. 'Do you love me?' In many ways Christianity has become an intellectual exercise which can split humanity apart. Many evil and twisted acts of bigoted anarchy were to be enforced in the name of Christianity and still are. 'See how these Christians love each other!' is a valid indictment. But please do not wipe out Christianity because there have been almost unforgiveable errors. As Jesus said 'If you are without sin, throw the first stone!'

It was always meant to be a love affair. That is the only thought that makes any sense of this Jesus business.

The Spirit of love is surely God's Spirit and it is ours. We are called to reflect the image of God in our lives … God's Spirit in us.

Many years ago a seafarer said to me, 'If you have the Holy Spirit, we should be able to see it!' And he was right. We are meant to reflect the love of God in our lives. At the end of our days, the value of our life can only be measured against the love that we have shared with our fellowmen. The day of judgement is today and we are judged day by day.

'I may have faith strong enough to move mountains;

but if I have no love, I am nothing'

1 Corinthians 13

Following in the steps of Jesus is a 'today' action. We only have the present moment. We cannot change what is past and we have no control of the future. 'If you want to put a smile on the face of God, tell him your plans for next week.' All that you have is the present moment, so get on with it.

'The harvest of the Spirit is love, joy, peace, patience, kindness, goodness, fidelity, gentleness and self-control.' Galatians 5.22-23

Good luck with your love affair!

It is said that Christianity is caught, not taught, and that is precisely the story of my life. Church-going was a natural activity in my family and that was where my journey began. There were no flashing lights or earth-moving visions. My life was a quiet, gentle and steady movement towards the ultimate statement ... Jesus is my Lord and my God.

That is the resurrection in me.

Charity No 224664

Charity No 220793

Liverpool Seafarers Centre is an ecumenical partnership between the Apostleship of the Sea (Liverpool) and The Mersey Mission to Seafarers. Based in Waterloo, adjacent to The Port of Liverpool, daily we visit all vessels berthed in the River Mersey and when resources allow, vessels berthed with the Manchester Ship Canal. Our work is very practical and much of what we do is pretty routine. Today, many Seafarers come from countries in the developing world, such as the Philippines, India, Ukraine and China. They work to send money to support their families back home. Being at sea for long periods means that Seafarers can loose touch with what is going on in the world. We supply summaries of the days news, often in the home language which is well received by all. Communication with family and friends is often difficult whilst at sea. It is not until the crew arrive at a port such as here in Liverpool that access to affordable communication, either landline or via the internet is possible. We encourage all Seafarers to take advantage of shore leave, when authorised, however with 24 hour, 7 day working, resulting faster turnarounds for the vessel, shore leave is at a premium. The Centre is a safe haven where the Seafarer can relax in comfort, enjoy conversation away from the constant noise and vibration together with all of the health and safety regulation. A game of pool or table tennis, have a beer or soft drink and replenish the stock of confectionary!.